perspectives
ON DESIGN
GEORGIA

Published by

PANACHE
PANACHE PARTNERS

Panache Partners, LLC
1424 Gables Court
Plano, TX 75075
469.246.6060
Fax: 469.246.6062
www.panache.com

Publishers: Brian G. Carabet and John A. Shand

Printed in Malaysia

Distributed by Independent Publishers Group
800.888.4741

PUBLISHER'S DATA

Perspectives on Design Georgia

Library of Congress Control Number: 2009922814

ISBN 13: 978-1-933415-68-0
ISBN 10: 1-933415-68-1

First Printing 2010

10 9 8 7 6 5 4 3 2 1

Right: Lisa Torbett Interiors, page 210
Previous Page: Mark A. Palmer, Inc., page 108

Panache Partners, LLC, is dedicated to the restoration and conservation
of the environment. Our books are manufactured with strict adherence
to an environmental management system in accordance with ISO 14001
standards, including the use of paper from mills certified to derive their
products from well-managed forests. We are committed to continued
investigation of alternative paper products and environmentally
responsible manufacturing processes to ensure the preservation of our
fragile planet.

perspectives
ON DESIGN
G E O R G I A

creative ideas shared by leading design professionals

introduction

Janet Powers Originals: a Gallery on Newcastle, page 226

Creating the spaces in which we live and achieving the beauty we desire can be a daunting quest—a quest that is as diverse as each of our unique personalities. For some, it may be serene hardscaped gardens; for others, it may be opulent entryways. Aspiring chefs may find a kitchen boasting the finest in technology their true sanctuary.

Perspectives on Design Georgia is an exquisite pictorial journey from conceptualizing your dream home to putting together the finishing touches, to creating an outdoor oasis. Alongside the phenomenal photography, you will have a rare insight to how these tastemakers achieve such works of art and be inspired by their personal perspectives on design.

Within these pages, the state's finest artisans will share their wisdom, experience and talent. It is the collaboration between these visionaries and the outstanding pride and craftsmanship of the products showcased that together achieve the remarkable. Learn from leaders in the industry about the aesthetics of a finely crafted sofa or how appropriate lighting can dramatically change the appearance of a room.

Whether your dream is to have a new home or one redesigned to suit your lifestyle, *Perspectives on Design Georgia* will be both an enjoyable journey and a source of motivation.

chapter one: the concept

chapter two: the structure

chapter three: elements of structure

contents

chapter four: elements of design

chapter five: living the elements

"Careful consideration of scale and proportion allows architectural and site opportunities to be seamlessly woven."

—Alec Michaelides

Wissmach Architects, page 56

Cutting Edge Stone, page 146

Berndsen Custom Homes, page 68

Michael Jackson Landscape, page 258

Turner Construction, page 98

Cutting Edge Stone, page 146

"Interior design is as much about people as it is about spatial plans, finishes and furnishings."

—Lisa Torbett

Cutting Edge Stone, page 146

François and Co., page 188

"Inspiration can come from an object,
a picture, a work of art, a sketch,
all of which aid us in building the
foundation for art while guiding us in our
development as artists."

—Keith Summerour

Dillon Forge, page 182

Berndsen Custom Homes, page 68

Wissmach Architects, page 56   Summerour & Associates, page 46

the concept

chapter one

Guided by architectural philosophies rooted in classicism and traditional detail, Harrison Design Associates has created residences of timeless importance and distinction since its founding in 1991.

As a young architect, founder William H. (Bill) Harrison journeyed to Italy, where he toured the buildings of renowned 16th-century architect Andrea Palladio. The experience left a lasting impression. Heavily influenced by the application of classical proportions, Bill displays an ardent respect for the purest elements of enduring architecture, apparent throughout his firm's designs. Contexualism is a vital design foundation; the firm's homes display a connection to their site, often culling natural resources for construction. Treating each new home, renovation or addition like a finely crafted work of art, a team of more than 85 architects and designers is on hand to meet the needs and lifestyles of each homeowner with an intensely personal design.

With offices in Atlanta and St. Simons Island, Georgia, and Santa Barbara and Beverly Hills, California, Harrison Design Associates implements site planning and landscape architecture, architectural design, interior design and construction administration and management.

"A home should incorporate a few unexpected elements that make it one-of-a-kind."

—William H. Harrison

HARRISON DESIGN ASSOCIATES

ABOVE: My personal home's site is especially meaningful as it's the property on which my wife grew up. I designed the home as an Italian villa in the Palladian style with respect to the land's natural elements. Palladio's influence is evident in the structural details and strong sense of proportion that pervades the home. Two symmetrical wings, one formal and one informal, flank a classically proportioned living room that is the heart of the home. This vaulted 22-foot-tall cubic room strikes a balance of proportions with the adjoining wings of the home and within the living room itself. A window organization of circles and arches inspired by Palladio's Villa Poiana lends additional architectural interest and connects the home with the surrounding woodlands.
Photographs by Emily Minton-Redfield

FACING PAGE: The five-part Georgian-style home applies classical symmetry and detailing in a formal Southern vernacular. The floorplan revolves around a central axis, producing visual destinations for the homeowners' collection of fine art and antiques.
Photographs by John Umberger, Real Images

PREVIOUS PAGES: So much of what will affect the design of a home comes from the property and its surroundings. The owner—a longtime family friend—and I searched for four years to find the right property for her family's dream home; when this seven-acre piece of land came up for sale, there was no question that it was perfect. The English manor home maintains an eclectic Arts-and-Crafts cottage feel. Although it presents a stately façade, the floorplan focuses on livable and inviting spaces. Designed to accommodate an active family, the back of the home features a combination of large windows and covered terraces that create a wonderful extension of living areas and allow the homeowner to supervise her children while attending to her other passion, gardening. By placing the informal and recreational rooms on the main level and connecting them to the formal spaces via a gourmet kitchen and keeping room, we've facilitated an effortless stream of interaction among all family members.
Photographs by John Umberger, Real Images

ABOVE: Located just off the beach at Sea Island, the Mediterranean Revival cottage incorporates Spanish, Moroccan and Italian influences. Drawing inspiration from the works of Addison Mizner, this design is characterized by simple forms and finishes punctuated by moments of deliberate ornamentation. Rooms relate harmoniously to one another rather than to a single axis, which underscores the organic balance. For example, a series of arched openings lead from the living and family rooms into the sunroom and on to another series of arched doors with Corinthian-style columns leading to the pool terrace beyond.

Photographs by John Umberger, Real Images

FACING PAGE: Our clients' passion for classical architecture is reflected in the European grandeur of their Italian-influenced seaside retreat. In a playful turn, we designed the principal rooms of the main level as a modern interpretation of an ancient open-air market with unadorned limestone columns, neutral plaster walls, 13-foot ceilings and arched mahogany doors and windows that open directly to the shore allowing breezes and sunlight to flow throughout the home.

Photographs by William Waldron

"Homes don't have to be complicated, just personalized."

—William H. Harrison

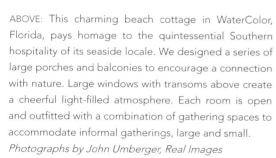

ABOVE: This charming beach cottage in WaterColor, Florida, pays homage to the quintessential Southern hospitality of its seaside locale. We designed a series of large porches and balconies to encourage a connection with nature. Large windows with transoms above create a cheerful light-filled atmosphere. Each room is open and outfitted with a combination of gathering spaces to accommodate informal gatherings, large and small.
Photographs by John Umberger, Real Images

FACING PAGE: Sitting high atop a concrete pedestal, a wall of fiber cement panels masks the support functions of the home, providing both privacy from the bordering road and a backdrop for the light-filled living areas. An overhead door and more than 800 square feet of additional glazing in the main living spaces provide an intimate connection with the river and surrounding national forest while belying the limitations of a 20-foot-wide buildable area. The constraint of an existing septic tank proved to be an excellent opportunity to create a sculptural elevated deck. At the far end of the deck, a hot tub sits atop two concrete pilings, creating a crow's nest vantage point from which guests may enjoy the views of the river and the home.
Photographs by Boutchine Studio

"A residence's connectivity to its site and locale, however slight or considerable, is absolutely critical."

—William H. Harrison

RIGHT: In the past few decades, Americans seem to have gotten caught up in the pursuit of bigger domiciles, yet homes have moved away from what made them special and unique: the symbiotic relationship between home, family and location. Our quest is returning architecture to its original intent, thereby improving homeowners' lives and the built world. A Mission-style Arts-and-Crafts Revival incorporated rock, quarried on site, as its major detail material. We oriented the home to take advantage of exceptional views of the harbor and cascading hillside. The arched area houses the exercise room, which takes one's mind somewhere else during an arduous morning workout.

Photographs by Jim Bartsch

FACING PAGE: It is very gratifying when we are able to incorporate materials indigenous to the site into our designs. A rustic, Shingle-style home had many surprising elements, which is directly related to the creative level of the craftsmen involved. The powder room walls are made of bark, not only an interesting visual, but a recall to the home's rustic location.

Photographs by John Umberger, Real Images

St. Simons Island off the breathtaking southern coast of Georgia is steeped in a history rich in building. Some four thousand years after the first inhabitants fished, farmed and hunted the island's inland, shores and marshes, colonial development began to leave thumbprints in the form of forts and missionaries. Later came quaint churches and lighthouses, and today, the current residents of St. Simons Island can take pride in the exquisite and masterful architecture that abounds throughout the community.

According to architect John Rentz, a leading residential designer on the island, first impressions are everything, and the entry is the beginning and most important part of the journey through a home. It must excite and energize, and a key component of any entry is the stair. For any stair to succeed it must be melodic. It must be playful and serious at the same time.

More than mere stone and mortar, architectural features such as the stair should be a clear and pleasing part of the total building composition. It should be a part of the total building whole; in successful architecture, that whole should be greater than the sum of its parts. Each part adds drama to the other. The sum of the parts make the whole we call architecture.

"The success of architecture is measured by a sense of place, belonging and meaning. Any successful entry should welcome."

—John R. Rentz

JOHN R. RENTZ, ARCHITECT

"The effective foyer must gracefully and poetically be an anchor or precursor to other spaces."

—John R. Rentz

RIGHT & FACING PAGE: Similar to the exterior entries, interior entries or foyers must logically meld diverse spaces together while hinting at other spaces. It is this melding of space that characterizes the pleasing contemporary lifestyle of today, a challenge to any residential architect in our time.

PREVIOUS PAGES: Effective composition of windows and doors, pilasters and columns seem to belong to each other. In both a spiral staircase and a curved balustrade, sinuous twists seem light and lyrical while commanding our attention with order and structure. *Photographs by Harlan Hambright Photography*

"If a beautiful outdoor feature is available, successful architecture will never deny it. If there is none, successful architecture will create one."

—John R. Rentz

RIGHT: The veranda and terrace both embrace the commanding view of the Atlantic on St. Simons Island. The fabric drapes at the veranda protect the interior from early sun. Likewise, the awning canvas protects the windows nearby from high noon glare to the living space inside.
Photograph by Harlan Hambright Photography

"Successful architecture will always merge interior and exterior space."

—John R. Rentz

ABOVE & FACING PAGE: Stained wood, stone walls, timbered beams and pillars and the warm wash of lighting play against each other to enhance various modulating spaces. The dining area extends through walls and merges with the outdoor screened veranda for additional alfresco dining while the interior living space merges with the dining area, simply and logically separated by the structure of beams and pillars.
Photographs courtesy of John R. Rentz, Architect

"The critical use of the foyer provides the formal recognition of entry that we still seek even in contemporary spatial planning."

—John R. Rentz

LEFT: The staircase creates diagonal interest along a formidable stone wall, accentuating the room's height and framing the commanding chandelier as the focal point of the open space.

FACING PAGE: The timber motif lends itself throughout the house. Thick and rugged ceiling beams play against masterful woodwork and floors, even furniture, giving the home a warm and comfortable while rustic ambience.
Photographs courtesy of John R. Rentz, Architect

Architects aren't mind readers—but the good ones sure seem like it. Kirkland + Associates is built around the idea of an ultra-customized, client-centric approach that aims to know homeowners as well as the architects know themselves. Extensive interviewing and in-depth lifestyle analysis give the team an edge; concept meetings, innovative problem solving and precise communication guide the process.

Founded by Patrick Kirkland more than two decades ago, the firm relies on a three-prong creative force to design its multimillion-dollar dream homes. Laura Potts teamed up with Patrick in 1992, when the practice took on a stronger residential focus and an environmental awareness, later to be joined by Karin Green. Each architect brings an impressive background to the practice and offers a distinct dynamic to every project. Patrick works closely with high-end communities and developers to gauge the appropriate style, size and overall approach to projects. Licensed in 12 states, Kirkland + Associates creates homes across Georgia, Florida, North Carolina and throughout the Southeast. The designs strive to make the homeowners' lives easier with close attention to site and scale. Detail-oriented and creative by nature, Kirkland + Associates thrives on high expectations and design challenges.

"Architecture is about volume, inside and out, and how spaces feel to a family."

—Patrick Kirkland

KIRKLAND + ASSOCIATES ARCHITECTS

"When a home is illuminated with warmth, the response is unanimous: Everyone feels comfortable."

—Karin Green

ABOVE & FACING PAGE: When a magazine featured Villa Bella Vista as its 2008 dream home, we knew it would sell fast. Purchased before construction had finished, the home takes its inspiration from Tuscan architecture found throughout California. The design features recycled timber beams, limestone fireplaces, gas lanterns on the porch and unobstructed views that make the home site-specific. A radiused wall of windows is unforgettable, bringing in views of green fairways and nearby water. But it's the hidden details of the design that make this home feel just right; the subtleties are what make people fall in love with it.
Photographs by Lauren Rubinstein, courtesy of Atlanta Magazine

PREVIOUS PAGES LEFT: The English manor responds to the slope of the land and tree cover within an ultra-exclusive gated community. Because the family is young, we went with an open floorplan that caters to practicality; the landscaping is intended to mature with the site.
Photograph by Paul Dingman, Dingman Photo

PREVIOUS PAGES RIGHT: Set in a golf course community, a Craftsman-style home includes brick, stone and cedar shake to achieve the look we intended and the homeowner wanted. Warm and welcoming, the home accommodates a couple who loves to entertain; designing a stunning entrance and catering kitchen was a must. The house shows off our technique of incorporating thoughtful solar orientation and window placement to include as much natural light as possible.
Photograph by Paul Dingman, Dingman Photo

ABOVE: Limestone, slate and mahogany define a countryside manor that seems more likely to appear on a European hillside than in an Atlanta community. We helped the developer size the lots to accommodate a wide range of architectural styles. A large home sitting on a double lot suited a long, narrow floorplan that emulated the vernacular of an English manor. Even though British architecture typically features dark woods and deep-toned rooms, we kept plenty of light flowing through the home by paying close attention to the depth and openness of the design.
Photograph by Paul Dingman, Dingman Photo

FACING PAGE: Privacy was a must because of the corner lot and its exposure to passersby. Following the land's cues to a perfect approach, we used a V-shaped floorplan that allows security and seclusion in the backyard.
Photograph by Gregg Willett, Gregg Willett Photography

ABOVE & FACING PAGE: Designing a 15,000-square-foot home on a constrained site gave us many opportunities to devise innovative solutions. In order to preserve a century-old beech tree, we designed the entire house around it and developed a linear floorplan that responded to the homeowners' programmatic needs. We not only spared the tree but managed to access views of the golf course without losing privacy and didn't encroach upon the wetlands beyond the property. Featuring vaulted ceilings, cypress and cedar, the family room offers a 56-inch fireplace and artisan work throughout. Wholly engaged in the process, the homeowners had an amazing ability to visualize the space and remained hands-on—always the best way to ensure a happy homeowner.
Photographs by Gregg Willett, Gregg Willett Photography

"A home isn't just specific to the homeowner; it's also specific to the land."

—Laura Potts

LEFT: Wouldn't you like to take all of this in? That was the notion behind our design of the radiused wall. A sloped ceiling and reclaimed distressed lumber add intimacy and character to the space. Potentially the darkest area of the design, the space above the kitchen needed clerestory windows to illuminate the room and show off the white wood that gives an easy rural feel to the kitchen. The most amazing aspect of this home, however, is its comfort. There's no pretension or ostentatious motive; everyone feels right at home.
Photograph by Lauren Rubinstein, courtesy of Atlanta Magazine

FACING PAGE: Resulting from a collaborative effort with the interior designer and homeowner, meticulous woodwork makes the room stunning and takes its inspiration from traditional English architecture. Extensive travels allowed the homeowner to integrate pieces from around the world, including cast-iron light fixtures, furniture and tapestries.
Photograph by Gregg Willett, Gregg Willett Photography

A youthful but experienced team of design professionals, Summerour & Associates has gained renown for the creation of highly detailed, aesthetically pure and richly crafted architectural projects throughout the Southeast. Auburn graduate Keith Summerour founded his namesake firm in 1991 with a keen eye toward the changing world of architecture along with an appreciation for and acknowledgment of timeless standards.

Keith emphasizes a holistic approach to design that considers architecture, interior design and landscaping in concert, resulting in harmoniously composed high-end residences, vacation homes and quality commercial projects. In January 2005, Keith founded Summerour Interiors in the same spirit and family atmosphere of the original studio to reinforce the importance of the essential relationship between architecture and interior design. The firm's main studio is set in a refurbished Atlanta warehouse overlooking Atlantic Station while rural studios include a stunning countryside tower in Gay, Georgia, and a studio/cottage in the mountains of Cashiers, North Carolina.

"Seeing a concept finally come to fruition is a joyous moment."

—Keith Summerour

SUMMEROUR & ASSOCIATES

ABOVE: Large doors open onto the wrapping porch, which greatly enhances the amount of usable space; for the best views—30 miles in any direction—the open-air, top-level observation deck can't be beat.

FACING PAGE: We designed the countryside tower in Gay, Georgia, to give our staff a wonderful rural studio in which everyone can get away from the hectic pace of city life. Inspired by my studies in Florence, the structure is truly rooted in the land and place.

PREVIOUS PAGES LEFT: The three-sided porch affords compelling views and space for outdoor leisure with protection from the elements.

PREVIOUS PAGES RIGHT: We used standing-seam metal roofs along with cedar driftwood timbers and balusters to create a rich, natural aesthetic for a rustic plantation home inspired by regional 19th-century architecture in Camden, Georgia.
Photographs by Jim Lockhart

"A home should be a utopia in which stress melts away."

—Keith Summerour

RIGHT: A mature live oak is silhouetted by a breathtaking sunset; outdoor fireplace and furniture make the rooftop patio an ideal setting of serenity.
Photograph by Jim Lockhart

"A well-designed space, even of generous proportions, exudes a sense of intimacy."

—Keith Summerour

ABOVE LEFT: Tremendous lake views abound when you lounge in the cozy hanging bed; the lamp made from a tree trunk fits in perfectly with the wooded setting.

ABOVE RIGHT: The screened-in dining area affords the sights, sounds and smells of nature in an engaging indoor-outdoor space.

FACING PAGE TOP: Alfresco leisure is the norm at a remarkable South Carolina residence set along Lake Keowee.

FACING PAGE BOTTOM: Connecting a variety of the home's interior and exterior spaces, the loggia, with its groin-vaulted stucco ceilings, is a marvel of design and craftsmanship.

Photographs by Jim Lockhart

"Inspiration can come from an object, a picture, a work of art, a sketch, all of which aid us in building the foundation for art while guiding us in our development as artists."

—Keith Summerour

ABOVE: Intended to replicate the bow of a ship, the terrace affords stunning views to the water; the louvered balustrade further conveys the nautical theme.

FACING PAGE TOP: A U-shaped pool area ties together two wings of the contemporary home; the circular windows of the changing room/poolhouse mimic those of a ship.

FACING PAGE BOTTOM: The dining loggia, just steps away from the pool, includes an inviting fireplace for winter as well as a ceiling fan for summertime outdoor recreation.

Photographs by Jim Lockhart

For Richard Wissmach, AIA, a love of architecture was borne from hands-on experience working with relatives to build homes as a youngster. This love of craftsmanship blossomed into an affinity for design and making all the pieces fit together as something beautiful, thoughtful and enduring. Richard's firm, Wissmach Architects, is a design-driven studio based in Savannah that responds to each project's unique conditions through a signature, collaborative design process melding context with innovation and professional expertise.

Recognizing the value of bringing as much expertise to the design process from the onset as possible, Wissmach Architects approaches every project as a communal undertaking between the client, interior designers, landscape architects, consultants and contractors. The results stand testament to the value of this approach: Wissmach Architects' work has been recognized regionally on television, in print and through the receipt of many AIA design awards. But it is truly the satisfaction of its clients that underscores Wissmach Architects' unwavering commitment to design quality.

"Things that are beautiful always contain just a touch of strangeness."

—Richard Wissmach

WISSMACH ARCHITECTS

"Architecture is a marriage of function and aesthetics— a careful blend of utility and beauty."

—Richard Wissmach

LEFT: An intimate screened-off porch between the homeowner's master bedroom and study is a wonderful place for respite, affording expansive views to the nearby marsh and Colleton River.

PREVIOUS PAGES LEFT: A holistic approach to landscaping, exterior architecture and interior design results in homes that harmoniously blend indoor and outdoor spaces in truly engaging compositions.

PREVIOUS PAGES RIGHT: Western red cedar shakes, brick and a standing-seam metal roof create a rustic aesthetic that is ideal for the wooded Bluffton, South Carolina, setting.
Photographs by Attic Fire Photography

ABOVE: On what was a fairly flat site, we created a gentle slope and elevated the pool and hardscape area; the brick wall demarcates the lap pool. The home's center mass is an open porch off the great room and dining room, and it is flanked by screened porches on either side; the poolhouse, Jacuzzi and outdoor fire pit complete the outdoor setting.

FACING PAGE TOP: Engaging vistas abound around every corner; the view from the kitchen through the dining area extends out to an open porch and summer kitchen with marsh scenery beyond.

FACING PAGE BOTTOM LEFT: The mudroom connects to the garage with a covered breezeway and is intended for storage of shoes, coats, umbrellas and other outdoor items; naturally finished pecky cypress siding and brick afford a rich aesthetic.

FACING PAGE BOTTOM RIGHT: The great room is adorned with gracious trusses and includes winsome views through the rear porch out to the water.
Photographs by Attic Fire Photography

"Our designs fundamentally start with the rich heritage of Southern vernacular architecture, which is then infused with contemporary materials and construction methods to create homes that are timeless in character yet functionally modern."

—Richard Wissmach

ABOVE: We elevated a portion of the rear yard to give the lawn definition for a beautiful home of parged brick with roofs of both slate and leaded, coated copper. The three center bays of the sun room, along with the dormer above, ensure that interiors are bright and welcoming.

FACING PAGE TOP: The vaulted, one-story great room is defined by natural materials like hard pine wood floors, painted cypress walls and brick, which also appears on the home's exterior.

FACING PAGE BOTTOM: We painted the brick walls in the kitchen but left a subtle accent of the natural brick to express the arch openings into the dining room. *Photographs by Attic Fire Photography*

"Integrated environments are created through thoughtful, responsive designs that are sustainable and highly contextual, thereby reflecting a unique vision."

—Richard Wissmach

ABOVE: For the 2008 HGTV dream home in the Florida Keys, we wanted to capitalize on the wealth of astounding views to the nearby Florida Bay. Indigenous materials like stucco, lap siding and a metal roof, along with a bright color palette, pay homage to Key West architecture.

FACING PAGE: The dining area is open to the kitchen while the master bedroom's porch affords stunning bay views; the stairs lead up to an elegant vestibule connecting to the master bedroom.
Photographs by Attic Fire Photography

Berndsen Custom Homes, page 68

Hixon Homes, page 78

the structure

chapter two

J.T. Turner Construction, page 98

Mark A. Palmer, Inc., page 108

Housing Trends, Inc., page 88

With a solid background in large commercial building projects and a degree in construction engineering, Jon Berndsen has spent the last couple of decades making a name for himself in the residential world, creating impeccably detailed, historically accurate homes throughout Atlanta. Berndsen Custom Homes is known for its wealth of design and building experience and its impressive caliber of projects. The firm spends a great deal of time researching and perfecting each architectural detail and was selected to be a founding member of the Southeast Chapter of the Institute of Classical Architecture and Classic America, an organization that promotes the value of classical and traditional design in creating high-quality built environments.

The Berndsen team works primarily on new construction projects but has also been commissioned to restore the work of celebrated classicists like Phillip Shutze, Neel Reid, Clement Ford, James Means and Lewis Edmund Crook. Jon and his team of craftsmen continue to be chosen by the area's finest modern-day architects to build the most challenging of residences.

"Classicist philosophies apply to all architectural genres. They are values that have stood the test of time through shifting architectural favor."

—Jon Berndsen

BERNDSEN CUSTOM HOMES

"With the right team, a family's home becomes a very important personal accomplishment for everyone involved."

—Jon Berndsen

LEFT: For a home so magnificent from the front, the back elevation could not disappoint. Large balconies create outdoor living spaces, which look out onto a tranquil outdoor oasis.

PREVIOUS PAGES: A blending of Beaux-Arts with Italianate Revival creates a striking approach. The united goal of the homeowners, architects and my team was to make the home appear as timeless as possible, as if it could have been built a century ago. We acquired the magnificently robust 12-foot front doors, circa 1830, from a palace in Paris. Abundant balconies add a romantic feel to the home while providing practical space for more entertaining areas.
Photographs by Jon Berndsen

"There are plenty of reclaimed and salvaged materials out there; using them benefits the environment and makes for brilliant, eye-catching details."

—Jon Berndsen

ABOVE & FACING PAGE: The flowing interior layout is in keeping with the classical design with large, high-ceilinged rooms aimed for entertaining. The overall goal was that the home look elegantly aged. We were fortunate to acquire salvaged antique limestone flooring from a large home in Italy; reconfigured antique gas and kerosene lamps; and reclaimed lumber, windows and doors that had been manufactured in France using centuries-old methods. Everything was related and anything more contemporary, such as some of the wood floors, was scrapped to add a charming patina. The millwork and details are appreciated every day by the homeowners, who feel incredibly fortunate to live in their dream home.
Photographs by Jon Berndsen

ABOVE: Italian Renaissance architecture blends facets of Italian Revival with Baroque details. Each balustrade has been hand carved and set in place. Although initially the difference between Old World techniques and contemporary "quick" method of creating these details may be undetected, close examination reveals the beauty of well-crafted details, and the long-term durability of tried-and-true methods proves that a craftsperson's painstaking effort is time well spent.

FACING PAGE TOP: We were fortunate enough to acquire antique oak for the entire library's masculine paneling from 600-year-old oak trees that had blown over in Versailles. The integrity and hue wrought by the age of the lumber yields a very rare wood with which to work. We were thrilled at the very rare discovery. The focal point limestone fireplace was hand carved in Italy.

FACING PAGE BOTTOM: The entire wine cellar is crafted from antique heart pine from 200- to 300-year-old trees. The wood has a golden honey color with red tint that you certainly cannot get from modern trees that haven't been given enough time to mature. After the 1920s, none of this type of pine has been available—another wonderful find.

Photographs by Jon Berndsen

"Never underestimate the impact of superior hand craftsmanship. Although we are a society of 'faster and better,' nothing compares to the quality and aesthetic beauty of hand craftsmanship."

—Jon Berndsen

ABOVE & FACING PAGE: The same home's rear elevation showcases its precise axial symmetry with a lovely view to the pool with very notably focused details. All of our work includes unexpected flourishes and hand crafted details. The hand carved entryway, balusters and lion's heads are no exception. It was important that the home be an accurate representation of the style but have nuances all its own as well.

Photographs by Jon Berndsen

Only one career path suited Jim Hixon, and he knew it before leaving college at Georgia Tech. For a man who loves to work with his hands, Jim naturally gravitated toward the construction industry at a young age. While he earned his degree, part-time homebuilding work began occupying most of his time—the more he built, the more he loved it.

Now, more than 20 years after it first began, Hixon Homes stands as a thriving business in the Buckhead area, providing residential and remodeling expertise. Although custom homebuilding dominated his portfolio in the beginning, Jim's focus turned to high end, high rise construction projects. Because of his specialty knowledge, Jim has helped establish a strong building niche with Hixon Homes, giving Georgia's upscale condominium owners the chance to live in the most customized space possible.

"Building within the limits of a high rise offers very different challenges than traditional homebuilding—the parameters completely change."

—Jim Hixon

HIXON HOMES

"It's important not to overstep your bounds while building a home. I let designers and architects do the drawings. I love to build, and that's what I do."

—Jim Hixon

RIGHT: Many of my clients have traded in their large homes for more intimate living quarters. For a retired Peachtree Street couple, we created a home that suited their lifestyle and reflected their refined taste. They purchased two condominiums within the same building, one on the east side and the other on the west. The designer connected them to create a gallery effect and show off the owners' extensive art collection. The carved marble fireplace, fabric walls and drapery design complement the construction of the space.

PREVIOUS PAGES: Situated on the seventh floor, the condominium reveals the life of its well-established resident. The space shows a simpler, relaxed environment. Strong aesthetics throughout demonstrate careful craftsmanship; detailed paneling wraps above the ceiling and adds an elegant effect. The walls are adorned with artwork from the owner's late wife, giving the home its character.
Photographs by John Umberger

"For the homeowner who's ready to build, there's no such thing as too much planning. Preparation equals efficiency."

—Jim Hixon

ABOVE: Defined beams and stone walls in the breakfast room give warmth and drama to the home. We used honed limestone tops, a custom stainless brass hood and dropped walnut for the island's back counter. Collected by the homeowner, antique English tiles dating back 150 years make up the backsplash.

FACING PAGE: My favorite part of the job is being in the field; I don't step on the designers' feet. And there's no reason I should since I've been able to work with some of the country's top names. For a home that features custom handrails with bronze accents, meticulous paneling and walnut floors, my close collaboration with the designer created impressive results.
Photographs by John Umberger

ABOVE & FACING PAGE: How do you turn a traditional, fourth-story space into a contemporary masterpiece? Plenty of manpower and solid problem solving skills. The two-story Atlanta apartment gave us a challenge when we installed the 5-by-11 stainless steel island. Quickly ruling out the elevator as an option, we hoisted the island top on the building's exterior, entering through the terrace doors. We transformed what once looked like the White House into a modern apartment using extensive glasswork and careful construction. Featuring tall glass pocket doors, switchback stairs, maple floors and automated shades that reveal treetop scenery, the interior now reflects the owner's taste.

Photographs by John Umberger

"The number of relationships we establish and the friends we make can sometimes get lost in a project, but really it's the most important element in the process."

—Jim Hixon

ABOVE & FACING PAGE: After running a side business that focused on carpentry and trim, I specialized in architectural details. And I used all of my know-how for a complicated seventh-floor penthouse. Espresso wood floors divided by large concrete tile make up the sleek floor. The fireplace features custom concrete pieces with a cantilevered hearth. Mahogany steps create an offset box look; their seemingly simple appearance was anything but. With the technical help of an engineer, we built the stairs with a metal post midpoint with a welded gusset to support the glass. Ceiling-high frosted glass allows light to spread throughout the space while providing privacy in the master suite. The kitchen uses the same elements—glass, steel, wood and light—to create a clean, modern setting.
Photographs by John Umberger, courtesy of Trends Magazine

Atlanta-based Housing Trends maintains that when designed and built to exacting standards, a house is not merely a home—it's a space that just feels right. Homes built by Housing Trends are unique and reflect the personalities of their owners. Founded in 1986 by Richard Clegg, Housing Trends specializes in custom building, remodeling and renovations of dream homes, taking a focused, calculating approach that ensures consistent quality.

Richard elaborates: "I realized more than 23 years ago that we couldn't deliver custom home value without a team of experienced and responsible people. A few hundred dream homes later, we continue to leverage the combined experience of our team to exceed people's expectations."

The firm's attention to detail and communication skills enable homeowners to enjoy finely built, richly crafted homes without the hassle. Housing Trends' unwavering attention to people is what distinguishes it from other skilled builders in the Southeast and enables clients to put their personal stamp on their most valuable possession while enjoying one of life's most satisfying experiences.

"Maintaining a connection between the home and its grounds is paramount."

—Richard Clegg

HOUSING TRENDS, INC.

"Thoughtful analysis and precise execution take the complication and mystery out of custom homebuilding."

—Richard Clegg

RIGHT: For a home on the river with a severe elevation drop, we strove to maintain the connection between the basement level, pool and master suite and to establish a sense of flow between areas. The beautifully designed home with historical influences inspired the material palette, which includes brick insets on the chimney, brick wings with lap siding above and composite limestone handrailing. The challenge is to combine timeless detailing with low-maintenance characteristics.

PREVIOUS PAGES LEFT: Added on during the renovation, the elevated porch is framed by stately white columns set atop Tennessee fieldstone supports and is one of the owners' favorite relaxation spots.

PREVIOUS PAGES RIGHT: The renovation project involved completely gutting the house and adding the front porch and garage structure. After discussions about whether to tear down the house, which featured a poor layout and underutilized spaces, we added doors and windows to establish better circulation between rooms.
Photographs by Jennifer Lindell

"Indoor-outdoor living has grown increasingly important in recent years."

—Richard Clegg

LEFT: While most wine cellars tend to be highly stylized and elegant spaces, they are most often hidden away in dark corners. The glass-covered hole in the kitchen's mahogany floor gives a hint of the wine cellar below in a novel way.

FACING PAGE TOP: Another engaging outdoor space enjoying shelter from the elements, the alfresco setting is defined by symmetry through the brick arch to the pavilion beyond and takes advantage of outlying views to the river.

FACING PAGE BOTTOM: Inspired by a historical mansion in Virginia, the dining room, with its elaborate wainscoting and compelling arched entry, is truly a work of exquisite craftsmanship.
Photographs by David Schilling Photography

ABOVE: In a very large room—31-by-56 feet with a 28-foot-tall ceiling—we wanted a cozy aura within an open-feeling layout. The combination of the size and placement of the furniture helps break down the scale for an inviting tone. The stone behind the fireplace provides contrast and visually defines the space.

FACING PAGE: I designed the staircase in collaboration with the architect, and we had a lot of fun with the design. We curved the stairs all the way up, which adds a sense of excitement and grandeur to the entry.
Photographs by Scott Moore

ABOVE: The elevation of the grand residence, one of our flagship homes, was developed over time from a collection of pieces; the combination of symmetry and classical elements makes it one of the most beautiful homes we've ever built.

FACING PAGE TOP: Rather than tucking the wine tasting room away on the lower level, we placed it on the main level, with easy access right off the kitchen; humidity and cooling considerations were more challenging in this configuration, but the space can be easily enjoyed by many.

FACING PAGE BOTTOM: Our favorite screened porch we've ever built, the space is ideally suited for outdoor living with a grill, fireplace, cypress ceilings and protection from bugs and the elements.
Photographs by Scott Moore

More than 30 years ago, while other builders and contractors developed new housing in the outskirts of Savannah, J.T. Turner Jr. led his new company down the less-chosen path of historic renovation. The bones of the century-old buildings stood the test of time as evidence of pride in craft; thus Jim modeled J.T. Turner Construction on the simple but critical notion that every element of a building should be remarkable.

J.T. Turner Construction is an award-winning builder, addressing both new and existing historic, custom and commercial construction while operating a 24-hour remediation management division. A J.T. Turner home is characterized by rich detail and extraordinary millwork, incorporating as many green principles as possible. The company currently has 12 LEED-accredited professionals as well as multiple LEED-registered and -certified projects. Jim Turner continues to incorporate the family business' core values and ethics learned from his two mentors, his father J.T. Turner and Hugh H. Armstrong. Integrity, client satisfaction, quality, service and dependability are the key values that have been the basis of the company's success to date. As son Tripp Turner prepares to lead J.T. Turner Construction into the future, he continues to preserve the legacy created by Jim Turner and his contemporaries during the previous three decades.

"It is always imperative that the architect and builder work as one with owners to achieve the vision they have for their finished product. Our goal is not to just create a structure but to create a home that is in harmony with its surroundings."

—Tripp Turner

J.T. TURNER CONSTRUCTION

"When a contemporary residence blends into a historic neighborhood, it's important for the new style to respect the existing architecture."

—Tripp Turner

RIGHT: The project predictably generated a good deal of interest in the downtown community due to its extraordinary design. It was, without reservation, unanimously approved by the Historic Review Board for its innovative design, appropriate scale and overall form. A recent recipient of a preservation award from the Historic Savannah Foundation, the custom residential project is comprised of reinforced masonry and steel with STO power wall stucco finish. The floor, roof and interior walls are conventionally framed, and the west wall of the house faces the garden. The residence has 45 Weather Shield windows overlooking a steel balcony and four massive rectangular columns. The house has a curved standing seam section that connects the guest bedrooms and bath above the garage to the main body of the house. Designed by Daniel Snyder Architect PC.
Photograph by Attic Fire Architecture Photography

PREVIOUS PAGES: The newly constructed pool pavilion is located on the historic Delta Plantation in South Carolina. The Georgian style seamlessly fits within the architecture of the historic main house. With abundant skylights and arched fanlight transom windows streaming natural light above and all around as well as a full-service kitchen and luxurious restroom facility, the pavilion provides an invigorating spot for a morning swim or a social gathering. Designed by Historical Concepts.
Photographs by Atlantic Archives: Richard Leo Johnson
Architectural Photography

"Custom residences deserve the finest materials. By incorporating premium finish materials to accentuate even the smallest of details, we can create unlikely focal points."

—Tripp Turner

ABOVE: Located at The Ford Plantation in Richmond Hill, a grand Southern home features double porches on the front and back façade, which overlook the surrounding mature landscape of majestic oaks, magnolias and oleanders.

FACING PAGE TOP: Directly behind the formal dining room, the full-function kitchen is adorned with travertine, granite countertops and distressed cherry cabinets. The baseboards surrounding the kitchen have a 12.5-inch base moulding.

FACING PAGE BOTTOM: The custom entry unit creates a formal living room area with clear cypress walls and Honduran heart pine floors. The hand carved wooden columns are situated on the four corners of the entryway, creating a grand entrance to the home. Designed by Hansen Architects PC.
Photographs by Attic Fire Architecture Photography

"What an honor it is to be able to restore these beautiful estates in downtown Savannah. It is very important that historic features are preserved while homes are renovated to accommodate modern amenities and lifestyles."

—Tripp Turner

ABOVE LEFT: Modern appliances mixed with classic detail comprise the kitchen, whose walls are clad with limestone. Sharing space with the kitchen is a casual family room and breakfast area.

ABOVE RIGHT: The extraordinary foyer of the home is illuminated with 19 neoclassical panels hand painted by a local artist. Each seam was custom designed for the foyer.

FACING PAGE: The beautiful Savannah estate, directly across from historic Forsyth Park, was originally built in 1909 for Georgia banking entrepreneur Mills B. Lane. It has received an award from the Georgia Trust for Historic Preservation and has been featured in numerous publications as well as the film, "The Legend of Bagger Vance." Designed by Hansen Architects PC.
Photographs by Atlantic Archives: Richard Leo Johnson Architectural Photography

"My father, Jim Turner, started his company by preserving the beautiful structures of Savannah's past, and we have completed over 250 historic renovation projects in downtown Savannah."

—Tripp Turner

LEFT: The William F. Brantly House is a fine example of attention to detail and quality craftsmanship. Side porches overlook the stunning views of historic Gaston Street and Forsyth Park. The terrace level, which had been partially enclosed, was reopened during the course of construction. A second level was added to the porch creating an outdoor space serving the master bedroom suite.

FACING PAGE TOP: A connector between the carriage house and main house was designed to provide access to the guest suite, which includes a bedroom, bathroom and sitting area. Too shallow to accommodate the length of a modern car, the ground floor was bumped out, and a veranda was created atop this addition.

FACING PAGE BOTTOM: We restored the amazing early 1800s John Norris home to its former splendor. The graceful plaster arch was recreated, and the ornamental plaster crown carefully restored. New marble mantels were carved to replicate the originals, which had disappeared in an earlier renovation. Designed by Greenline Architecture.

Photographs by Atlantic Archives: Richard Leo Johnson Architectural Photography

Custom. It's the byword of the acclaimed homebuilding company Mark A. Palmer. Now under the guidance of Alan Palmer, the firm creates many of Atlanta's most luxurious residences, each of which is completely unique. Projects are replete with reclaimed flooring, custom millwork, elaborate stairways, intricate mouldings and anything else the architect and homeowner can dream up. The team is proud to declare that what they build and craft can't be found in a catalogue or on the shelves of a store.

In order to achieve the level of detailing that is synonymous with the Palmer name, the team works to produce, review and redraw the building documents until every last element is perfect in the eyes of everyone on the project team—especially the future homeowners. Equal attention is given to the aesthetics and what lies beneath the finely finished surfaces because this custom homebuilder constructs homes to not only last but also to age gracefully and be timeless contributions to the neighborhood's architectural fabric.

"You want a home to be so strong, well-built and meticulously detailed that in 100 years it fully deserves a renovation."

—Alan Palmer

MARK A. PALMER, INC.

ABOVE & FACING PAGE: It is up to the custom builder to put all of the pieces together and to be sure that they fit. Our homes use combinations of reclaimed wood and natural materials such as bluestone and limestone, and all of it must seamlessly tie the home together to maintain the architectural intent. To achieve this, the materials used on the exterior of a home are often mirrored in the interior.

PREVIOUS PAGES LEFT: Millwork is critical in giving a home charm and uniqueness; an empty wall becomes a focal point when beautiful cabinetry is built in, a mantel becomes a work of art and a ceiling gains admiration.

PREVIOUS PAGES RIGHT: Although technically a renovation, nothing original was left on the outside of a traditional brick and stone home. All materials used are authentic. Manmade materials like cast stone, while potentially cost saving, tend to be lacking in detail. An elegant home relies on the integrity of its materials and methods. The Leuders buff-hued limestone details are produced locally from quarried blocks of stone.

Photographs by John Umberger

"A timeless home is one that's designed specifically for the people who will enjoy it and built to the highest standards."

—Alan Palmer

RIGHT: Originally clad in dark-stained cherry wood, the library now boasts white-washed cypress milling, which offers a complete departure from the expected. Light and cheerful yet still substantial, the space engages the natural light and palette for a refreshing change. And leaving no detail unaddressed, the bricks are laid in a herringbone pattern inside a full masonry fireplace.

Photograph by John Umberger

ABOVE & RIGHT: Unique, beautifully executed millwork is a theme in all of our homes. Homeowners desire to make a mark that renders the home all their own—from the family room to the library. Our extraordinary craftspeople accomplish this with each project. Originally an open porch, the space was turned into a library for a former owner by architect Philip Trammel Schutze. As part of the most recent renovation, modified woodwork accommodates artwork over the fireplace for the current resident with new cabinetry added to one wall as well. Importantly, original stain was matched as part of the intent that all changes should appear to be original. A shallow coal-burning fireplace was rebuilt from the outside in order to be made deeper, allowing for wood burning; the original mantel dictated the dimension. Part of the beauty of a true masonry fireplace is complete flexibility in dimensions.

FACING PAGE: The homeowners came up with the idea of barrels and had them fabricated in California; they're a charming addition to the entertaining wine room.

Photographs by John Umberger

"Photographs let you in on the structural beauty of a project, but they speak nothing of the intense collaboration required to get to that pristine state."

—Kathy Gregorcyk

ABOVE & FACING PAGE: Originally designed by architect Jimmy Means, a 1960s residence underwent recent renovations designed by Rick Spitzmiller and Robert Norris that included a family room, kitchen and garage addition. The new gallery graciously unites the additions with the original rooms and allows for much more natural light throughout the space. The stair hall is part of the original Jimmy Means design while the gallery and living room can be seen through the cased opening. The new family room opens into the kitchen, the gallery and a screened porch, which include very private views onto a landscaped backyard and woods that are part of the large piece of property beyond. The family room walls are paneled, the ceiling is finished with ship-lapped poplar boards and the fireplace wall is brick unified in the same color. All of the residence's fireplace hearths were built on site using plaster.

Photographs by John Umberger

"Mixing manmade and natural materials creates dynamic designs."

—Teri Duffy

elements of structure

chapter three

S tyle. Everyone wants it—from clothing to art to interior design. But is it something you are simply born with, or can it be acquired? Teri Duffy is a living example that it takes both nature and nurture to achieve a strong sense of style.

As the granddaughter of an artist and the daughter of a designer, Teri knows that her talents run in the family. Her daughter has even followed suit, becoming a designer like the generations before. But formal education and experience in the field have been just as important as natural abilities. With a Bachelors of Fine Arts and nearly 30 years in the business, Teri has made T. Duffy & Associates one of the most reliable names in Georgia's interior design industry. Her spaces are clean, elegant and eclectic, always capturing the essence of the site. Light and scale take center stage—two critical elements that can bring a room to life. No two spaces are the same, and each demands something different from Teri. She blends the old with the new to reach the vision of the homeowner, always achieving strong, fresh, inviting spaces.

T. DUFFY & ASSOCIATES

"Successful design mixes simplicity and attention to detail for both decorating and architectural elements."

—Teri Duffy

LEFT: Interior architectural elements and site-specific details are critical when designing—I always pay close attention. The rhythm of the kitchen's beams carries through to the office, which maintains this strong element while allowing the office to evolve as its own space. For a straightforward, quiet master bedroom that faces a lush golf course, artwork by Ron van Dongen lends depth. And a master bath with a teak tub and bench play off of the mosaic-tile shower. The flush floor creates interest and offers a smooth transition. All of the elements of the space work together for a clean, refined look.

FACING PAGE: Using a theatrical element in an otherwise minimal space reinforces juxtaposition and creates a wonderful curiosity. For a sitting room, the focal point is an antique sailboat. The result: warm, comfortable, contemporary. Outdoor views became the second focal point because the space faces water, bringing the coast lifestyle indoors in a sophisticated way. Clean lines and a soft palette define the room.

PREVIOUS PAGES: The uniqueness of a project can be its original construction. A traditional home became contemporary when the owner wanted to stay with the existing lot and floorplan. We used integral-color concrete floors and created a fireplace with built-in niches of sheet rock and thick wenge wood shelves.

Photographs by Atlantic Archives, Richard Leo Johnson

"My mom has endless energy and passion for creating spaces that are chic and livable."

—Megan Duffy Hamilton

ABOVE LEFT: We redesigned the master bedroom to combine the character of the past with eclectic furnishings and contemporary artwork of today.

ABOVE RIGHT: Space constrictions were our main challenge when making a small area into a master bath suite. We lifted the roof and reconfigured the tub, closet, shower and toilet area while floating the vanity cabinet for more room. It is a highly functional space but small, so we chose lavish materials to make up for that fact. Marble, grass cloth and high-end fixtures give an exquisite feel. Oak scalloped cabinetry shows off careful craftsmanship.

FACING PAGE: A kitchen remodel included two pairs of antique walnut doors that lead to the pantry and show off one-of-a-kind detail. Since the homeowners loved bold colors, we used them in the adjoining breakfast nook for a dramatic effect. The fun colors stand out, complementing the green walls and neutral colors in the kitchen. A shiny purple synthetic fabric was chosen for the custom banquet to contrast with the antique metal French table. The drapery is green stripe horsehair fabric, accenting the kitchen walls. Reiterating the interest of texture in a space is equally as important as the furnishings themselves.
Photographs by Joel Silverman

"People's passions, collections and hobbies are the ultimate creative inspirations."

—Teri Duffy

LEFT: Two antique Chinese art pieces served as the inspiration for our palette in an urban residence. Bringing in natural light, the large window highlights the gardens; the dining room opens to the living room, staircase, galleries of antique artwork and wet bar. Beautiful aged transfer tiles from the homeowner's collection dating from the late 18th century gave us the insight we needed to design the kitchen. The tiles are displayed as the backsplash and reveal the essence of the space. Also featuring Old World elements, the staircase displays family portraits from the 16th, 17th and 18th centuries.

FACING PAGE: A black marble fireplace and light-blue glazed walls exhibit contrast within a neutral palette. The layering of art, textures and accessories lends additional depth to the space.
Photographs by John Umberger

"A space that juxtaposes timeless luxury with contemporary minimalism creates a stunning environment."

—Teri Duffy

ABOVE: The hallway located in a high-rise residence uses architecture as a strong interior design element. A series of arches leads to family seating that opens to the kitchen. A Swedish canopy is mixed in with antique furniture and contemporary artwork.
Photograph by Gerlich Photography, Fred Gerlich

FACING PAGE TOP LEFT: Our inspiration for a powder room came from delicate hand painted wall coverings. A custom, lacquered blue vanity stands out next to the refreshing view of the plaza's in-town gardens.
Photograph by John Umberger

FACING PAGE TOP RIGHT: Set above the treetops, a lake-facing master suite took on the feel of a cozy nest as we placed a three-quarter-foot wall half way into the room and laid the bed in its own niche. With a color scheme inspired by the surrounding nature, the home's walls are stained shiplap white pine with antique wood floors.
Photograph by John Umberger

FACING PAGE BOTTOM LEFT: When we began working on a guestroom dedicated to children's friends and that adjoins to the play area and living room, we knew we could have fun with the design. Some of the accessories include antique oars and quirky French artwork while the orange palette gives off warmth and whimsy. Exaggerated height and rich, orange raffia-covered headboards make the guest feel embraced.
Photograph by Chris Voith

FACING PAGE BOTTOM RIGHT: We designed an in-home wine and tasting room for a Georgia family—the results are stunning. An antique Belgian storefront door serves as an entry to the cellar and is complemented by the tufted leather, ceiling-high banquette seating. On the opposite side, an antique table and three tabourets provide a lounging area. The finishes used in the wine cellar are primarily stone, antique beams and refurbished hardwood flooring.
Photograph by Gerlich Photography, Fred Gerlich

"Design is a reflection of timeless style."

—Teri Duffy

TOP: Because we had limited space, recessed wenge wood bookcases adorn the walls, and seating faces the TV and antique desk. The room opens to a hallway collection of black and white photography and gives the illusion of a bit more space.
Photograph by Atlantic Archives, Richard Leo Johnson

BOTTOM: Set in a 1950s' sunroom-turned-dining room, an Alvin Booth art piece is featured alongside a 1940s' floral etched and beveled mirror.
Photograph by Atlantic Archives, Richard Leo Johnson

FACING PAGE: For a lady's bathroom that overlooks the park, we chose custom cabinetry in a light-antiqued aqua with a herringbone marble floor. From our artisan, a custom-made mirror sits in front of the window—a touch that I often use.
Photograph by John Umberger

"We refine the world's most sophisticated home automation technology to enhance and simplify life."

—Rod Laserna

ABOVE & FACING PAGE: Ultra customized and designed around the homeowner, our installations offer seamless home integration with the most innovative technology. For a lodge-style recreation room, we designed a system that allows the family to adjust every element according to their needs—whether it's a relaxing movie night or an evening of high-stakes billiards.

Photographs by John Umberger

"Home automation can work for any family. It's just a matter of finding the right systems to fit your lifestyle."

—Rod Laserna

LEFT: Some of the best spaces in the house are outdoors, which are ideal for entertaining and hanging out. Enjoy your outdoor living space with the sounds of music, a ball game or a movie of your choice from your private collection. Whether you are indoors or out, music and video entertainment is available from your media concierge.

FACING PAGE: We take the intimidation out of technology. We make certain that every homeowner understands just how straightforward our designs really are. One control unit centralizes the home's system and brings a highly energy efficient, streamlined approach to monitoring the house. Imagine running everything with ease, with a single touch-screen control—lighting, music, televisions, security and HVAC from one location. Convenience is priceless.
Photographs by John Umberger

"Our systems are designed and structured to give people the ability to adapt to new technology in a way that avoids obsolescence."

—Rod Laserna

ABOVE: The home theater isn't just a place to watch movies; it's a place to escape. Designed for the entire family to relax, the room offers every type of comfort imaginable and places a whole new perspective on the way you live.

FACING PAGE: We gave a contemporary space a technology makeover, offering an entertainment system that matches the sleek, clean appearance of the natatorium. A waterproof remote in the pool adds to the seamless integration of the design; no detail was forgotten.
Photographs by John Umberger

"Why go out to the movies when you can bring the theater into your home?"

—Rod Laserna

RIGHT: We take home theaters to the next level. Plush seating and architectural detailing add to our media systems for an unforgettable cinematic experience.
Photograph courtesy of Automated Lifestyles

FRANCOIS AND CO.

Atlanta, Georgia

"The essence of our design philosophy is the combination of architectural statements, exquisite materials and passionate master craftsmanship."

—Thierry Francois

ABOVE: Inspired by history, we've been traveling to France for more than a decade to source one-of-a-kind antique mantels that are significant because of their unique past and stunning workmanship. Our flagship showroom features a large selection of antique period reproductions as well as contemporary mantels. We commission artisans who are experts in preserving stone works of art; understanding and capturing the original message from a long-gone artist—down to the tiniest stone detail—requires a passionate carver.

FACING PAGE: A great representation of a renaissance mantelpiece, the mantel boasts impressive proportions, sturdy pilasters, scrolled capitals and elegant entablature.
Photographs by Thomas Watkins

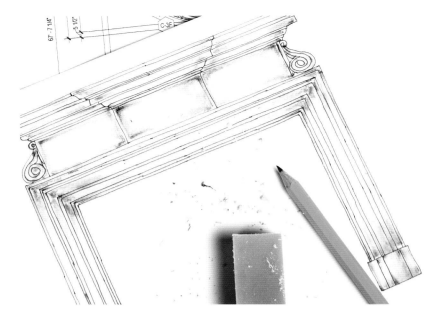

"The creation of a period reproduction starts with the acquisition of an antique masterpiece, which is then given to the most talented stone carver who can preserve the integrity of the original artist's intention."

—Thierry Francois

LEFT: We follow the best tradition of hand sketching and room rendering to introduce a concept and work closely with designers and architects to bring projects to life. The Carlisle mantel is one of our latest English period pieces. Illustrated by Olga A. Wildman. *Photographs by Laurent Cavalie*

FACING PAGE: Exhibiting an unsurpassed dedication to craftsmanship, our French carver begins sculpting a corbel following the all-time tradition of "chisel, hammer and sweat." *Photograph by Thomas Watkins*

RIGHT & BELOW: Combining the expertise of our designers, the variety of our textures and the quality of our finishes, we go to great lengths to create stretches of versatile and distinctive architectural details—such as our range hoods, which add an element of structure and style to any culinary setting.

FACING PAGE: Master craftsmanship and spirited soul bring design vision to life.

Photographs by Thomas Watkins

"Every bathroom is a sculptural opportunity that begins with a design feel and ends with embellishing details."

—Thierry Francois

LEFT: Our custom mosaics are defined by a spirited soul, skillful craftsmanship and marvelous coveted materials.
Photographs by Kevin Roman

FACING PAGE: The foyer exudes a classical feel with help from many architectural stone elements such as columns, moulding and wall cladding; even the flooring is polished French limestone.
Photograph by Thomas Watkins

Alpharetta, Georgia

"Some of Georgia's most beautiful homes display our stone work. We like to think our portfolio is scattered on the Georgian landscape."

—Bruce Koop

ABOVE & FACING PAGE: For estates that require dimensional limestone, we use state-of-the-art CNC machinery. All of our work is done to exact architectural specifications to create a noble, distinguished look.
Photographs by John Umberger, Real Images Photography

"Stone is an incredible medium. It's strong, stately and still captures intricate detail."

—Don Koop

RIGHT & FACING PAGE: We take classic architectural elements and blend them with contemporary design to create one-of-a-kind homes. Arched entryways, columns, fireplaces and window sills are adorned with Old World elements and a new-age feel. Inside our 40,000-square-foot plant, you'll find ultra-modern technology and nearly every stone tool our craftsmen could need, giving us unlimited options. We can create virtually anything.
Photographs by John Umberger, Real Images Photography

"The work of a good craftsman is timeless."

—Jessica Koop

ABOVE & FACING PAGE: One of the greatest qualities of stone is how well it blends with other materials. It complements wood, iron and any shade of brick. Whether we're fabricating a simple pool deck or an ornate exterior elevation, all of the elements have to work together to create a successful look.
Above left & facing page photographs by Kevin Kennally
Above right photograph by John Umberger, Real Images Photography

"Whether we enjoy cooking or not, we always find ourselves in the kitchen. It is the most used room in the house and absolutely critical in relation to the rest of the home. I call it the central hub, or brain, of the home."

—Cynthia Ziegler

ABOVE & FACING PAGE: During more than two decades of designing kitchens, I have witnessed the transition of the kitchen from a singularly focused room into a multifaceted hub of activity that on any given day serves as office, family gathering spot, cooking center, art room and more. Today's kitchens call for the perfect balance of functionality, versatility and aesthetics. I believe that it is vital to thoroughly explore and understand people's unique aspirations, objectives and lifestyles in order to create spaces that satisfy all of their specific requirements while conveying their unique style. An accomplished cook needed a total kitchen redesign, so the space was redesigned to take advantage of the beautiful garden views and create storage particular to her needs. I added a lot of details within her cabinetry to maximize functionality. I designed deep spice and utensil drawers and a small sink into the island—created to look like a table but function with specific storage needs—near her 48-inch commercial range. The stainless surface on the island makes for easy clean-up. Interior design by Carter Kay Interiors.
Photographs by John Umberger

"Per square foot, the kitchen is the most expensive room in a home. Many of a kitchen's elements are permanent and therefore must be thoughtfully laid out to satisfy your personal needs."

—Cynthia Ziegler

ABOVE: A historic 1918 Buckhead home required an entire renovation to make it functional for an active family of five. The homeowner admitted to me that although her kitchen was large, it did not work for her. Removing the huge metal hood that hung over the island and divided the room instantly created a view and much needed connection into the adjacent family room. The pantry was so far away it was virtually useless. By relocating the appliances, creating pantry storage closer to the cooking center, and designing specific cabinetry, I was able to meet all of my client's needs. A new sink was located under new corner windows so that the owner could see her family's comings and goings outside. The island now functions as an eat-in workstation for supervision of the children's homework or simply a visiting spot while the evening meal is being prepared. The homeowner expressly wanted a second oven placed where her children could peek in on baking cookies, and a bar was added where the old pantry existed. Interior design by Nancy Fallon Interiors.

FACING PAGE: Because the homeowner entertains often, I included two large sinks, plenty of workspace and increased refrigeration and freezer space. I kept the layout very open for multiple cooks or caterers. However, the owner still wanted a warm and intimate feeling for her family when not entertaining. With this in mind, the specific cabinet and appliance layout was critical so that this one space could function well in two different modes. Interior design by Nancy Fallon Interiors.
Photographs by John Umberger

"The kitchen plays many roles within the home and must be personalized and aesthetically pleasing. It must fulfill all of the residents' many needs, which is why guidance is so important when considering each detail of that room."

—Cynthia Ziegler

RIGHT & FACING PAGE: The joy I get from my work comes not when my clients tell me how beautiful their new kitchen looks, although that is important, but more so when they tell me how well it functions for them. I like knowing that I have made their life easier, more enjoyable and aesthetically more pleasing because the kitchen is where everything happens, and when it doesn't work, then everything is made more difficult. Here, I worked with the mother of four busy boys, ages 12-17 years old, whose kitchen needed an entire overhaul. The original space had no context to the rest of the home, the sink faced the back wall instead of taking advantage the family room view and the cabinetry was completely non-functional. Although utilitarian, kitchens must have the desired overall feel and look of the rest of the home for seamless cohesion. This kitchen missed the mark on two fronts: Context was the first issue, and the second, of course, was function. I changed the work triangle, improved storage space and, most importantly, designed the island to incorporate the eating area, which consequently brought it to the center of the room. Because it seemed a unique arrangement, I asked the homeowners to move their table to the proposed island area and just live with it for while to see how it worked for them. As I had hoped, they gave me the go ahead and today love how it brings their family together. Whether the family is entertaining friends, watching television, doing homework, enjoying family meals or just hanging out, it's the perfect spot to encourage daily interaction. Interior design by Alice Cramer. *Photographs by John Umberger*

"Natural stone is always a timeless choice and has been used for ages. In the hands of a skilled craftsman, there are very few limits to the uses of this material."

—David Webster

ABOVE & FACING PAGE: One my greatest privileges has been working with top professional designers, architects and contractors. These professionals have a vision and desire to reach beyond the realm of simple design, to create something lasting and unequaled.
Photographs by David Webster

"It's those little details and finishing touches that make a tile installation spectacular."

—David Webster

ABOVE & FACING PAGE: Timeless classics like Carrara marble basket-weave floors, subway tile walls and slabs of elegant Botticino marble lend to the ambience of tranquility.
Photographs by David Webster

"Shop for natural stone the same way you would a diamond. They are products of nature, and the quality is easily seen in both. Invest in quality materials that really reflect your taste."

—David Webster

ABOVE: High traffic areas can be as durable as they are stunning. We installed beautiful natural stone in a family's foyer that wows guests and lets the homeowners rest easy.
Photograph by David Webster

FACING PAGE: Our material selection gives the clean, crisp feel of elegance to a classically appointed powder room.
Photographs by David Webster

"We spend so much time in our homes that they should be truly reflective of our personal sense of style."

—Denis Duchesne

ABOVE & FACING PAGE: A 1914 Buckhead residence required a new architectural program that would do justice to its historic grandeur. The elaborate columns are complemented by three-part acanthus-style mouldings over the stove. The armoir-like enclosure houses the refrigerator, proving that a space even as utilitarian as a kitchen can be an elegant extension of a home's overall design.
Photographs by Michael Shir

"Specially designed millwork is definitely a focal point. It can completely transform any architectural shell."

—Denis Duchesne

LEFT & FACING PAGE: The terrace level's aesthetic is an intentional departure from the rest of the home. The adobe Arts-and-Crafts style features a naturally beautiful integration of ribbon mahogany and timber woods. Each section in the terrace is delineated by its distinct ceiling variation to create a free-flowing design. The Art Deco-influenced home theater is masculine and commanding in regal detail, beginning with the ceiling. Though it is a secondary living space, the area has a decided presence in the home and is the perfect space for informal and formal entertaining. Although my company's name may not say it all, I've designed everything from kitchens to whole-home interior architectural detailing.
Photographs by Michael Shir

"World travels can really inspire a home's detailing. You can blend the aesthetic of beautiful things you've experienced into a style that's uniquely yours."

—Denis Duchesne

TOP: A sleek, modern his-and-hers bathroom features smoked glass countertops and bird's-eye maple cabinets that are robust in hue and shape.

BOTTOM: A more traditional kitchen strikes a balance between furniture and cooking spaces.

FACING PAGE: Though much of my work features very eye-catching traditional design, I also enjoy and am experienced in the contemporary genre. The kitchen is a great place to explore modern design, even within a shell that has historically rooted style.
Photographs by Michael Shir

"It takes patience and determination to work with metal until the perfect design is achieved."

—Steven Schoettle

ABOVE: I believe every detail of a structure should have a connection. In the same way it has a connection, the structure also serves to complement the metalwork. Whether the design is an ornamental addition or a part of the built-in structure, my goal is for the ironwork to be a seamless connection to the space. I enjoy opportunities to design and build unique chandeliers as much as I enjoy playing an integral role in the aesthetics of a French-inspired kitchen. The copper range hood was a collaborative venture with Readdick Sheet Metal.

FACING PAGE: Part of my job is to alter people's perspectives on metal design elements. For example, the second-story skylight rosette seems delicate but is actually 24 feet square made of hand forged hammered steel. I welcome a challenge; it gives me the opportunity to find out what I can get from the metal and often broadens my range of thinking and creating.
Photographs by Sandy Schoettle

"It is amazing to see the various personalities metal adopts with each different treatment."

—Steven Schoettle

LEFT: People are often surprised to learn that not only will I design and fabricate built-in iron elements, but I also build completely unique metal and wood furnishings from floor and table lamps to four-poster bamboo beds. The entertainment center consists of one piece of forged steel surrounding the door panels made of reclaimed, antique barn lumber. I chose contrasting chestnut for the interior shelving, and to bring the piece together, I designed and fabricated steel hinges and door pulls with a finish to complement the steel body. I believe contrasting textures is a good way to create interest.

FACING PAGE TOP & MIDDLE LEFT: When I say I enjoy a challenge, I believe my work supports that. Clients of mine designed their seaside home with a nautical theme; however, when they asked to have actual rope rather than wood for their stair railing, building code would not allow it. So instead I weaved copper in an alternating pattern and applied oxidizers to give it a verde patinaed finish. Carrying the theme throughout the home, I created a twisted iron rope railing in a staircase leading out to a widow's walk overlooking the ocean.

FACING PAGE BOTTOM LEFT & RIGHT: Whether utilitarian, as in the case of a star rail, or ornamental, as in the case of an entry arch, metal is one of those natural materials that is surprisingly versatile. It can showcase a formal polish or rustic patina and has a personality all its own.
Photographs by Sandy Schoettle

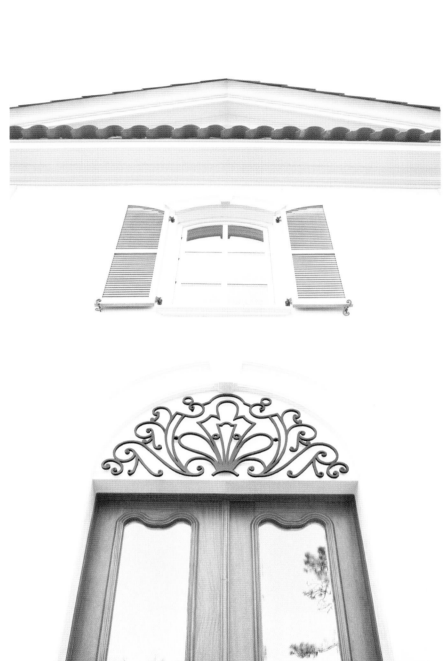

"Artfully applied oxidizers can completely transform the look and feel of a piece from contemporary to Old World or anything in between."

—Steven Schoettle

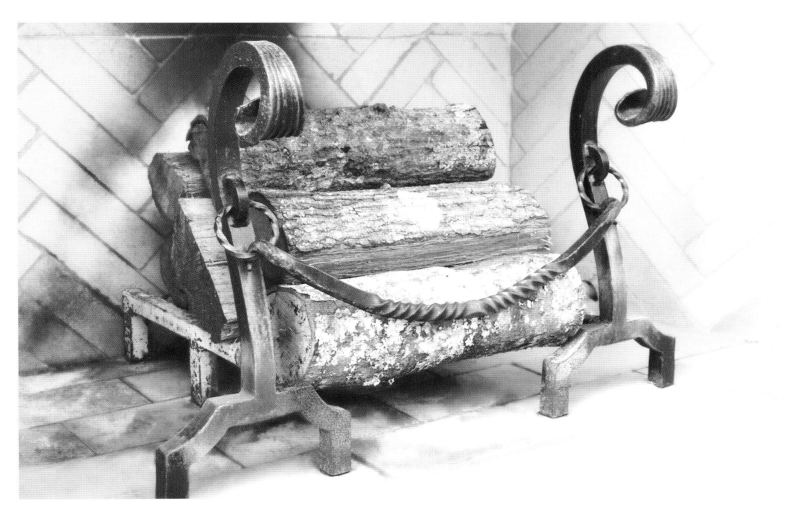

ABOVE: Usually there's a pretty involved design, development and approval process, but the andirons for an outdoor fireplace went from my head to chalk drawings to metal. Fiddlehead ferns in the courtyard inspired the inverted radius shape.

FACING PAGE: It's critical to understand where and how the ironwork will be installed before the designing and forging begins. The balcony's scrollwork extends upward, uniting the iron motif with the lighting fixtures and window, and because the piece takes cues from a French antique displayed inside, it also melds the indoor-outdoor aesthetic. Knowing that the lighting rosette would be viewed from a distance, I used oxidizers to add tonal interest. I designed the picket of the wine cellar window's ironwork to act as a foot bolt, allowing it to open for easy maintenance.
Photographs by Sandy Schoettle

"Understanding the architectural integrity of a home and a passion for wood species is what begins the creative process."

—Kevin Phillips

ABOVE: A lightly distressed and glazed solid cherry plank top nicely complements the cabinetry.

FACING PAGE: The choice of solid, durable maple for paint-grade doors— also proven warp resistant—and all-wood box construction provide the basis for quality work. Time-honored craftsmanship, a keen understanding of period and the intelligence of modern-day function is how a room becomes the favorite place in a home.
Photographs by Kevin Phillips

ABOVE & FACING PAGE: Skilled artisans create custom stains and glazes as executed in the island constructed from white oak. Color and scale of a piece can cleverly accentuate the diversity of space while custom mouldings and differing door styles create a blend of character and beauty.
Photographs by Kevin Phillips

"The presence of wood in the home is a soft-spoken reminder of our innate relationship with nature."

—Kevin Phillips

RIGHT & FACING PAGE: With color specified to replicate the stained and glazed finish on the handrail of the grand staircase for the original Saks Fifth Avenue in Atlanta, the woodwork of an elegant private library boasts moulding of intricate design, custom milling and hand applied finish. Behind the beautifully crafted panels is found computer and office equipment storage as well as the integration of a fully appointed bar with ambient lighting.
Photographs by Kevin Phillips

DILLON FORGE

Atlanta, Georgia

"It's impossible to rank form and function. All of the elements have to work together."

—Michael Dillon

ABOVE: The French design of a residential gate conveys the scale and grandeur of the entrance. With its massive size, 16 feet by 18 feet, the project required as much brute force as it did detailed artistry.

FACING PAGE: Our work fits into any environment. Set on the 53rd floor, an Art Nouveau loft needed installations that were as expressive as the work showcased within its walls. Overall, the results reveal fluid design that fits the space perfectly.
Photographs by Max Birnkammer

"A good blacksmith needs three things for success: a hammer, high heat and plenty of intuition."

—Michael Dillon

RIGHT: Our railings blur the lines of art and architecture in a historic home. Inspired by a Samuel Yellen window, the design of the ironwork shows keen rhythm.

FACING PAGE TOP: Both the arrow railwork and the Conway Manor project show our ability to fit and finish an installation with the highest level of precision.

FACING PAGE BOTTOM: Our French railings fit the architecture of the space. Graceful lines and touches like the bronze finial and elaborate volute stand out to a passing eye.
Photographs by Max Birnkammer

"Reclaimed wood adds a piece of history to a home; it is recycling in its most beautifully simplistic form."

—Wendy McGrew

ABOVE: When spaces include diverse, rich woods, the mood is instant, as seen in the distressed cherry cabinets and ceiling details. We installed tidewater red cypress in the living room's existing coffered ceiling and stained it a warm, rich color; the lighter flooring is an antique red and white oak, which has beautiful color variation. Although it may initially make some people nervous to use different wood types in one space, once they see the effect and the uniting elements we thoughtfully mingle, they are delighted. The dominating amber color throughout all the wood types is what allows them to work together. Demonstrating the difference a stain can make, the living room and library have the same cherry wood paneling, but the wood in the library has a hand rubbed wax finish. The antique oak flooring really ties the space together and makes a beautiful setting to catch up on some reading.

FACING PAGE: We specialize in antique lumber to deliver the authentic look that people desire. Robust 150- to 200-year-old lumber was reclaimed and transformed into expansive trusses, adding dramatic architectural elements to the home's keeping room and kitchen. Although it is a new residence, it has an Old World feel.
Photographs courtesy of Distinctive Building Materials

"Wood has character and life. Treatment of the wood, whether by stain, wax or paint, enhances its personality for all to enjoy."

—Wendy McGrew

ABOVE & FACING PAGE: Hand hewn timbers create a decorative element and provide structural integrity. Antique timber can have more strength than contemporary timber because the trees were allowed to mature before they were harvested. Over time, this century-old wood becomes even denser, making it perfect for sturdy use.
Photographs courtesy of Distinctive Building Materials

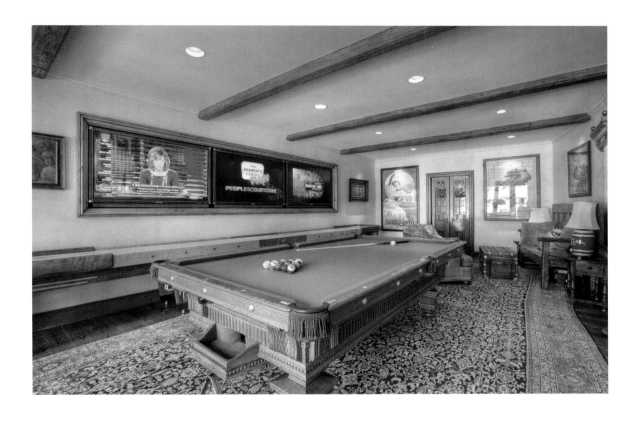

"Well-designed home electronic systems essentially give us more of our most precious resource—time."

—Trey Brunson

ABOVE: We installed three 65-inch screens—a modern addition to the playroom—allowing the residents to watch multiple games simultaneously and complementing the length and dimensions of an antique shuffleboard. The complexity of audio and video control is intuitively and easily managed by remote.

FACING PAGE: To preserve the traditional interior design element of the living room, a motorized system safely slides a painting to reveal a flat-screen television. Simple to operate, the system is controlled by the push of a button.

Photographs by Joe Loehle, EOJ Inc: Design & Photo

"Integrated systems, portable devices and digitizing sources can really maximize the management of large, modern homes."

—Trey Brunson

ABOVE: Uplighting accents and centralizes the home theater's concave, coffered ceiling, which is detached from the floor above with sound isolation springs. Located just below the home's library, the soundproofed room features an anamorphic screen, digital projector and acoustically transparent walls—the speakers are actually inside of the walls, and sound plays through cloth without any distortion.

FACING PAGE TOP LEFT: Included as an element of the room's design, a fiber optic ceiling emulates the movements of the universe and can bring up constellations and shooting stars, making the low ceiling a positive influence instead of a negative.

FACING PAGE TOP RIGHT: A 50-inch plasma behind a two-way mirror allows for entertainment during meals. The sound system is in the wall, so the speakers are not visible and can be sheet rocked or wallpapered over.

FACING PAGE BOTTOM: When viewing demands surpass the limitations of a 40-inch liquid crystal display television, a 123-inch motorized screen and projector drop from the ceiling. The system is supported by five channel surround sound, and the room's lighting dims automatically when the screen comes down.
Photographs by Joe Loehle, EOJ Inc: Design & Photo

"Design is the difference that turns a good project into a great project."

—Dove Brown

ABOVE LEFT: The custom-finished desk in the family entrance is the central nervous system of the house. The pink hue from the seat of the chair is mirrored in the center cabinets' pink fabric, which is held in place by chicken wire; beadboard backsplash between the extended corbels affords contrast and interest.
Photograph by John Umberger

ABOVE RIGHT: For the master bath in a Buckhead high-rise remodel, the homeowners were looking to make a dramatic statement. With limited space for cabinetry, we added architectural elements by creating the arch detail over the mirror. The unique mullion doors with antique mirror on the linen tower bring style and interest to this utilitarian piece.
Photograph by Chris Little

FACING PAGE: Knotty alder cabinets with a tumbleweed finish, along with cedar paneling on the walls that wraps the entire space, give a strong log cabin feeling to the terrace-level kitchen. To further accentuate the rustic aura, we used twig and acorn cabinet hardware along with a cattle yoke light fixture over the island.
Photograph by John Umberger

"Functionality is of paramount importance; so many beautiful kitchens are largely unusable."

—Dove Brown

LEFT: An array of cabinets defines the kitchen, which has many layers of richness. A variety of rectilinear forms gives the space great definition while the variations in the heights of the cabinets and range hood, as well as the material and color differentiations, give the room a warm complexity and interest.
Photograph by Chris Little

FACING PAGE TOP: The elegant kitchen is the result of a compromise of sorts; he wanted dark-stained cherry while she wanted a painted finish. Aesthetics aside, the increased functionality has encouraged the wife to spend much more time cooking.
Photograph by John Umberger

FACING PAGE BOTTOM: A deft mix of beauty and function, the kitchen is both refined and usable. The large white cabinets behind the island front a walk-in pantry and refrigerator; the drawerfronts at the ends of both sides of the island contain hidden electrical outlets while the columns flanking the oven and pantry conceal kitchen items.
Photograph by John Umberger

LINDER SECURITY SYSTEMS, INC.

Atlanta, Georgia

"Home theaters and security systems are now more practical than ever, and because the technologies have evolved so much, they're available to nearly every homeowner."

—Tad Linder

ABOVE: Home theaters aren't limited to the living room. Our systems can fit a multiuse space for any lifestyle through close collaboration with the architects and interior designers. For a room that functions as a conference area, den and full home theater, thoughtful planning makes it all work. When the retractable screen goes up, the space is transformed into a peaceful seating area. The lowered screen suits business needs and provides optimal viewing for films and video games.

FACING PAGE: We helped turn a pool house into the ultimate hangout spot. Whether guests want to mingle at the bar or watch the big game, they have full-view access throughout the space. Audio and visual integration gives the homeowner complete control over the large screen, three small screens and laptop computer. The large LCD screen works in any space with loads of natural light, preventing glare as the sun pours through the windows.

Photographs by John Umberger

"The design of a home security system should be based on a family's concerns. If we don't address their worries, then we haven't installed the right system."

—Tad Linder

RIGHT: Homeowners should think about what they want to accomplish with their security system. Protect property? Children? A valuable art collection? The answer is different for every home. For larger estate homes, we use security applications that include photoelectric beams and sensors that extend to the perimeter of the property. Camera systems allow residents to monitor any section of their home from anywhere, including remotely. Whether you need to check on the teenagers or make sure your pet is safe, out-of-town trips become less stressful with the right technology.

FACING PAGE TOP: For a homeowner who didn't want to sacrifice shelf space, we created a minimized system and blended the television screen into the bookcase. From here, he can control all home automation: HVAC, lighting, security, films and music.

FACING PAGE BOTTOM: Organization is key. It maximizes the user-friendly potential of our equipment. A universal remote places full control of home automation into one device. Space cannot be taken for granted in limited settings, and that's why we use it so efficiently. A hidden screen with smaller speakers achieves the quality of a dedicated home theater while maintaining an orderly appearance. Equipment racks also offer a one-stop control panel, centralizing the technology to a discreet location.

Photographs by John Umberger

"Wrought and cast iron work gives people the chance to bring a piece of history into their homes. The art form dates to 3500 BC."

—Igor Lipko

ABOVE & FACING PAGE: How can you capture 16th-century France in a home's interior? That was my challenge as I created wrought iron railings throughout a private residence. By using up-to-date technology with detailed European design, I modified the railings to suit the style of the home. Bronze and metal, used in different thicknesses, convey the look of French architectural details.

Photographs courtesy of Lipko Iron Work

"Don't overlook the craftsmanship of a blacksmith when designing a home. Our work adds to the appeal of any structure."

—Igor Lipko

ABOVE: To create a coffee table with character, I pulled heavy metals from a Civil War-era factory in Atlanta. Surviving more than two centuries in the downtown steel tower, the metal scraps had accumulated layers of rust and tarnish. I cleaned, cut and worked with the pieces in different phases to form an ornate, eye-catching table.

FACING PAGE: The design for a wine cellar door and rail work within a contemporary home came from an unlikely source—water. I turned forged metal into a pattern that mimics the look of a stream; leaf patterns and swirls can be identified throughout. The homeowner wanted to include the feeling of nature in the home's eclectic mix. Difficult to weld but easy to look at, the work was recognized with a top award in an international competition.
Photographs courtesy of Lipko Iron Work

OLDE SAVANNAH FLOORING

"A custom wood floor should act as the canvas for the rest of the house, not the focal point."

—William Riley

ABOVE: Like all of our floors, the American black walnut plank flooring in random widths and lengths was made-to-order for a private country club. We lightly hand scraped the wood, acid washed it then added two layers of custom color and seven coats of hand rubbed oil finish to achieve these remarkable results.

FACING PAGE: For a traditional living room, we came in and sketched out the room to get the correct scale for the chevron pattern. The quartersawn white oak flooring was prefinished at our shop—hand sanded, colored, sealed with an English sealer and hand waxed. Because the room is small, we wanted a lively pattern, so the boards are short and narrow.
Photographs by Brian Willy

"A timeless custom floor should pull a house's architecture and interior design together."

—William Riley

LEFT: Burmese teak flooring in a chevron pattern with a custom border unites the condominium's interior design elements.

FACING PAGE LEFT: The interior designer brought us a picture. We worked with it to create a pattern from plainsawn antique white oak—hand buffed, colored and rubbed with multiple coats of oil.

FACING PAGE RIGHT: Wood flooring is an enduring feature that adds warmth and softness to a house. For a bedroom, we lightly wire brushed northern white ash with a light colored wash then finished with a hand rubbed oil.
Photographs by Brian Willy

"Interior design is as much about people as it is about spatial plans, finishes and furnishings."

—Lisa Torbett

elements of design

chapter four

The arts of pencil with sketchpad and mouse with computer have never coexisted more happily than at Lisa Torbett Interiors, which has been gaining momentum and acclaim since the early '80s. Lisa found a fast friend and design counterpart in Dee Simmons and invited her to become a partner in 2007. Their philosophies are similar enough for smooth collaboration yet diverse enough to keep things interesting.

Over the years, they have amassed extensive experience with luxury resort and private club design, which has translated beautifully to their signature high-end residences. They know the best resources and always have their eyes wide open for inspirational pieces.

Although choosing a paint color can, indeed, be a daunting task, interior design is about far more than that. Sure, the walls are the canvas, but there are so many elements to consider—scale, texture, pattern and style, among others. When all of these aspects are thoughtfully developed, they weave a rich tapestry. This is a guiding philosophy for Lisa and Dee.

LISA TORBETT INTERIORS

"Allowing family heirlooms to inspire a room's composition or palette allows homeowners to instantly connect with their new space."

—Delinah Simmons

ABOVE & FACING PAGE: The whole home is grandly scaled with 18-foot ceilings, so while we're usually trying to make a room feel bigger, here we wanted to celebrate the volume but bring the window treatments and furnishings down to a more human—yet still luxurious—scale. In the dining room, we began with the fabulous print that now upholsters the chairs; it's bold, fun and reflects the family's personality. The multicolored silk drapery panels and custom rug amplify the colorful statement. We paid homage to the family's Heisey heritage by displaying a number of Heisey glass pieces on the shelves of the music parlor and a few in the breakfast nook and master bathroom. The powder room demonstrates the family's sense of adventure; the antique Venetian mirror hangs above a plaster vanity with marble top and charming wooden doors.
Above & facing page top left photographs by John Umberger
Facing page top right & bottom photographs by Howard Lee Puckett

PREVIOUS PAGES: Solariums are generally adorned with bright, colorful patterns that become even more intense with full sun. We chose an understated color palette with wonderful textures that invites people to linger. The architectural pecky cypress beams, engaged Corinthian columns and series of Palladian windows frame several seating areas, each defined by a rug, woven chairs and plush pillows.
Photograph by John Umberger

"Of course a room can change with the seasons. By creating a neutral palette punctuated by boldly colored accent pillows, accessories and artwork, seasonal updates are a breeze."

—Lisa Torbett

TOP: Each design is, and should be, a unique expression of its residents. Styles are across the board for us, but a lot of what we do has a clean, transitional aesthetic—the perfect blend of comfort, sophistication and timelessness. In the living room off the solarium, we used the painting's flora and coloration for inspiration points that led to solid and patterned bronze pillows, crème-tone upholstery and a delicate orchid on the coffee table.

BOTTOM: We whitewashed the pecky cypress ceiling and dangled airy iron light fixtures from it to illuminate the Oushak rug, majolica, French antique server, alabaster lamps, slipcovered hall chairs and oil painting of the coastal area. To make a vacation home feel like a true getaway, we like to incorporate the creativity of local artists.

FACING PAGE: In a well-traveled couple's living room, we showcased their passion for unusual objects with global treasures from contemporary art to ancient calligraphy pens.
Photographs by John Umberger

"Design is all about collaboration—between client, designer, architect and whoever else is contributing to the creative process."

—Delinah Simmons

ABOVE & FACING PAGE TOP: If you steer clear of trends and choose pieces with classic lines, patterns and coloration, the design can forever look as though it were designed yesterday. The cleverly upholstered dining room chairs' silhouette complements that of the sofa. Likewise, the graceful curve of the silk sofas echoes the arched doorways and moulding detail. The lightness of the silk and elegance of the needlepoint pillows draw attention to the fabulous Aubusson rug.
Photographs by Harland Hambright

FACING PAGE BOTTOM: Heirlooms like the oil paintings, bronze and crystal candelabras, porcelains and gilded mirror lend an established air to the new residence. The soft, buttery yellow walls are perfect to keep people visually engaged by the rare pieces.
Photograph by John Umberger

"The fastest way to make a room feel cozy? Add a beautiful rug."

—Delinah Simmons

ABOVE LEFT: Full of Moroccan charm, the covered porch with unobstructed views to the marsh and cozy fireplace inspires a "kick off your shoes and stay a while" mindset. The seating area doubles as an alfresco dining area. The residents just set the kilim pillows aside, slide the cushions to the floor and lounge around the table. The sun and moon dapple light through the trees for a romantic effect.

ABOVE RIGHT: When rooms have generous volumes, scale is absolutely critical. Working with a two-story space, we chose a fabric pattern with a medallion motif that would have seemed excessively large on its own—it's just right in context. We're so accustomed to scaling pieces that we usually know exactly what a room needs, but we've used everything from design software to plywood mockups to confirm that everything is perfect.

FACING PAGE: Old World charm at its best, the combined dining and living space feels light despite the heavy ceiling beams. We chose the chandeliers—each nearly five feet in diameter—because they're true to the wrought-iron character the room demanded but don't look too weighty. Generous windows connect the interior with the marsh filled with mature live oaks. Further linking the interior with nature, the antique barley twist chairs are upholstered in an organic motif.
Photographs by John Umberger

"If you want a smooth home design process, invite an interior designer to collaborate with your architect from the very beginning. You'll save time, money and energy, and the result will undeniably be better."

—Lisa Torbett

ABOVE: A bed is often the most challenging piece of furniture to select. It can't be too feminine or too masculine, and it needs to be unique and interesting since it's an obvious focal point. The arch-top chinoiserie bed makes good use of the high ceiling. Adjacently, the master bath suite's doors pocket into the wall, connecting the sculptural bathtub with the courtyard, which exudes a Zen-like quality, referencing Eastern cultures. At the far end, a shower doubles as a fountain or water feature. Furthering the indoor-outdoor connection, black granite floors the entire space.
Photographs by John Umberger

FACING PAGE: The entryway is eclectic in style and content. The Asian console, zebra rug and antique mirror keep the composition clean yet interesting.
Photograph by Howard Lee Puckett

C LIGHTING

"The key to lighting design is approaching it in layers."

—Yaacov Golan

ABOVE & FACING PAGE: As a lighting designer, I make it my objective to develop layers of light into every project. The best lighting plan incorporates function, form and flexibility. First, you need effective illumination then artful or decorative elements and, finally, the ability to adapt it all to the mood of the environment. Lighting plays an important role in how people feel; it's critical that my C Lighting team and I build every plan with this in mind. Interior design by C.B. Miles, Miles Design Inc.
Photographs by Parish Kohanim, Parish Kohanim Photography

"Every light fixture has a job to do, whether it's bathing a space in ambient light, drawing attention to artwork or brightening a workspace like a kitchen island."

—Yaacov Golan

ABOVE: Kitchen islands and countertops are spaces where task lighting is needed. Illuminating the task, directional light can be provided by down lights or lamps.

FACING PAGE: Don't forget windows as part of your lighting—the placement of pendant lights next to a wall of windows isn't mainstream, yet it's quite intentional. As the sun goes down, the room naturally transitions to an evening scene because the light continues to emanate from the same direction. Decorative fixtures such as a bedroom flush-mount should be considered objects d'art and not the primary source of illumination. Display lighting is used to highlight paintings, sculpture or an architectural interior. Track lighting or rail systems are an effective tool here. Wall surfaces are very important in bouncing and diffusing light. A matte finish in a soft color provides the ideal condition for playing with light. As the last step in any lighting plan, each element should be reviewed for its purpose; whatever does not provide function or form enhancing the space should be reconsidered. Finally, the proper installation of controls allows the space to be adapted to fit the appropriate mood. Interior design by C.B. Miles, Miles Design Inc.
Photographs by Parish Kohanim, Parish Kohanim Photography

JANET POWERS ORIGINALS: A GALLERY ON NEWCASTLE

"Rather than just documenting the landscapes as they are, my paintings are meant to portray a mood."

—Janet Powers

ABOVE: Consisting mainly of palms, "Buzzard Island" is reminiscent of the tropical southern coast. Soft edges at the tops of the palms suggest a gentle breeze blowing through the fronds.

FACING PAGE: "Into the Twilight" illustrates the soft muted colors of the day's fading light when the marsh grass takes on various shades of glorious warm glows.
Photographs by Janet Powers

"Simplicity allows an artist to be more of a poet than a novelist."

—Janet Powers

LEFT: Capturing the breathtaking calmness and natural beauty of the Golden Isles, three scenes rendered through monochromatic color schemes evoke the serene mood of the coastal marshes. In "Darien River and Marsh" the river creates a nice horizontal movement as the marsh recedes far into the distance. The sunset in "Mouth of Fancy Bluff" yields an intense aura, both in color and in warmth. The rich, muted monochromatic colors of the marsh grasses and the economy of shape allow "Mellow Morning Marsh" to enjoy ultimate simplicity.

FACING PAGE: The interplay of shades and color in oil paint brings the sky to life. In "Andrews Island Sunset," the blue sky juxtaposed with the orange sky sets up tension and vibrancy—predominantly dark values make the glow of the setting sun more eminent. The pinks and blues of the "Christmas Sunset" contrast with the earth tones of the marsh while impressionist clouds lightly float in the sky.
Photographs by Janet Powers

"A lot of inspiration comes from American and European architecture from the past, design motifs that have been used throughout the centuries."

—Joyce Eddy

ABOVE LEFT: Framing the fireplace with a design and finish that complements and reflects the style of other pieces in the room, the mantel is one of our architectural elements that fits into the interior design of the house.

ABOVE RIGHT: A converted sideboard, the master bath vanity anchors the room, providing a regal surface to display antiques. The hand painted design reflects a casual French, feminine atmosphere.

FACING PAGE: Consistent with the Grand European Casual lifestyle, hand painted and finished pieces such as case goods furniture—occasional tables, a mirror on the mantel and an armoire—blend seamlessly with antiques, upholstery and other pieces, uniting the great room's overall décor style. Our skilled craftsmen employ a unique multi-step finishing process to get the layered look and distressed quality of a true antique.
Photographs by Rob Brinson

"Livability and art should coexist not only to benefit the home but also to honor the tradition of artisans from days long past."

—Joyce Eddy

ABOVE: Exuding the feel of grand European French Country lifestyle, the kitchen showcases our cabinetry as well as our custom doorway entry, a solution for grand scale architectural elements—custom panels and shelves built as an architectural extension of the kitchen's design.

FACING PAGE: Barstools provide good examples of how mixing and matching finishes provide interest. The lighter finishes brighten the room, keeping the space feeling open, while the dramatic black tones and hand painted elements on the Venetian hearth make it a very stylistic and casually elegant focal point for the room.

Photographs by Tim Glover

"Your home should hold an ambience that means comfort to you. We constantly come up with unique ways to use faux finishes because comfort holds a different meaning for everyone."

—Joseph Schmucker

ABOVE: Crumbled Venetian plaster creates an intricate wall finish of smooth stone relief texture. The use of Venetian plaster is an Old World treatment, yet the palette makes all the difference. Used as an accent wall or the entire space, it makes a stunning backdrop for decorative details.

FACING PAGE: Different glaze or faux paint treatments can personalize a room, even a kitchen. We carefully consider customizing our bedrooms and family rooms but often forget that although it is wholly utilitarian, the kitchen is a very important personal space, too. Through the use of a light staining technique, new kitchen cabinets are given a sense of time. Within that vein of thought, we often breathe new life into dated kitchen cabinets through various paint treatments that revive and highlight the strong points in the existing cabinetry. It's also much more cost effective to work with what the home has than to replace cabinetry altogether.
Photographs by Joseph Schmucker

"When minds are opened to the possibilities of decorative finishes, the options are literally almost endless. People immediately think walls and cabinets, but once they see examples of faux finishes on floors, doors, furnishings, framing, moulding and more, the ideas start to flow."

—Julie Stoner

ABOVE: We choose color palettes that complement the decorative and architectural details of our clients' homes. Faux finishes and complementary colors may be utilized to showcase beautiful ceiling details, or gilded frame treatments may be used to show off a beloved art piece. The use of color allows one to appreciate its beauty alone while visually pointing out what the eye may not have readily noticed in the room's surrounding elements. It is also important that our work create a better world for our homeowners while respecting the world, which is why we choose to only use materials that are water-based, low VOC that do not create harmful waste or strong fumes.

FACING PAGE: Part of the appeal of diverse paint treatments is that we can compose washes to resemble almost anything within imagination. Expertly constructed furniture and heirloom pieces hold sentimental and real value. We always consider this when custom designing paint treatments for everything from a wash on a built-in cabinet to the whimsical paint design and treatment on a family's cherished 80-year-old hutch. Our goal is to enhance and add more interest to an already striking piece of furniture, wall, ceiling or home's architectural elements.

Photographs by Joseph Schmucker

MYOTT STUDIO

Atlanta, Georgia

"Maintaining the value
and condition of a piece
of art begins with sound
conservational methods used in
the framing process."

—Myott

ABOVE: Elton John's Atlanta residence is, as one would imagine, quite a unique showplace of art and style. The collection of photographs, though similar in tone and feel, vary in size. The choice of a uniform frame allows the series to be displayed in a manner where the artwork could be enjoyed without seeming chaotic.
Photograph by Charlie McCullers

FACING PAGE: In this interior by Epperson Design, the painting by Myott was intended to be a focal point in the room. With that in mind, we created a frame that would be both substantial in size yet delicate in finish so as not to overshadow the artwork. The beveled profile of the frame drives the viewer's eye inward, while the outside edge sits off the wall, creating a floating effect. The silverleafed finish was given a warm glaze to complement the subtle tones of the art.
Photograph by Chris Little

"A frame should not overpower or compete with the art, but rather enhance it. In the end, it's all about the art."

—Myott

TOP: This iconic photo commands a lot of attention. We advised the owners to create a niche within their book collection to showcase this image. The classic shape and size of the frame was chosen to complement the elegant pose of the fashion model subject.
Photograph by Charlie McCullers

MIDDLE: Contemporary paintings require very minimal framing for enhancement. The solution is simplicity. A frame was constructed with cherry wood ebonized to create a warm black. The style, known as a floater frame, provides a breathing space between the frame and the art.
Photograph by Deborah Whitlaw Llewellyn

BOTTOM: Location often plays as important a role in deciding the frame design as the art. The frame features a hand carved motif as whimsical as the photograph and hangs on a mirrored set of closet doors in the guest suite.
Photograph by Charlie McCullers

FACING PAGE: One of the recent trends in photography is to print in large scale, as seen in Eric and Bonnie Fishman's residence. The poignant photograph of a woman's face measures over 5 ½ feet tall. Although a minimal frame would have sufficed, it would not have had the visual impact and interest that the larger frame provides. We chose to create a grand scale traditional frame to play on the portrait-like pose of the model. The sensual curves of the moulding offer a feminine touch to a massive frame.
Photograph © Schilling Photography

VLOEBERGHS STAINED GLASS STUDIO

"Leaded glass
is a wonderfully
diverse medium,
and its popularity
through the ages is
a testament to its
timeless aesthetic."

—Patricia Vloeberghs

ABOVE: I consider myself an architectural leaded glass designer. My classical work is showcased all over Atlanta and from coast to coast. After a three-year apprenticeship in leaded glass repair and 30 years in business, I have learned where stress points are; I always use reinforcement systems in my work. When designing glass for such a vast area, specifically the 10-foot high by 5-foot wide bath window, I make sure there is structural support. To break down this large area into manageable leaded glass sections, I designed the iron frame and then my blacksmith, Michael Dillon of Dillon Forge, fabricated it. Featuring two types of textured glass and restoration glass, the Greek key border has 550 pieces in it. The center panel showcases mouth-blown Rondells cut into squares to obscure view. The top transom is hand rolled restoration glass from Germany. Restoration glass is made to look like glass from the 1800s and has so much life it actually seems to breathe.

FACING PAGE: I absolutely love it when my customers turn me loose and allow me to design something in a classical pictorial style. Inspired by the my client's special connection to dogwoods, "Dogwood Over a Lake" becomes all the more poignant. I enjoy using large areas of beautiful opalescent glass balanced with high detail. I "paint" with the texture and color of the glass to bring my landscapes to life. I gain inspiration from nature and often bring natural substances into my designs—geodes, agates and shells. The dogwood centers feature cabochons; the corners are dazzling slices of agate.
Photographs by John Umberger

"The huge distinction among glass is truly amazing. Even if one is not trained to know what the difference is, one simply feels and experiences it."

—Patricia Vloeberghs

LEFT: The desire for functionality and safety resulted in a beautiful design that met both needs. The leaded glass panels, installed in frames behind the ironwork of the doors, open to allow fresh air in while leaving the door secured. I ensured that the leaded panels line up with the ironwork exactly yet, when open, throw lovely shadows on the wall. I enjoy developing original solutions for my clients, and I never repeat patterns—I "twist" them a bit so each is an original.
Photograph by John Umberger

FACING PAGE: My work tends to fall into a traditional, historical looking aesthetic. I can design in any classical genre and enjoy making each panel unique in its own way, often by adding Rondells, cabochons or my hand crafted lead castings. To create my lead castings, I first sculpt the piece to be cast, make a mold then smelt the lead and cast in the mold. Each casting is then hand trimmed and soldered onto the leaded panel. In some instances, an interior presentation, I hand goldleaf each casting; all other castings have a pewter finish. To achieve an antique look (bottom left), I hand antiqued new mirror and then cut the antiqued mirror into my design pieces to be built into the leaded transoms. The design is complemented by hand goldleaf castings.
Photographs by Brian Gassel

"Every implemented design should exhibit a passion for creating spaces using bold and graceful design elements that are influenced by the home's architecture."

—Kenneth Lemm

living the elements

chapter five

L and Plus Associates, Ltd. began in 1985 with the professional collaboration of Kenneth Lemm, ASLA, and Alec Michaelides, ASLA, a synergistic relationship that has established Land Plus as one of the Southeast's most highly regarded landscape architecture and planning firms. The firm's portfolio includes an array of projects ranging from private residences and multifamily residential developments to specialty resorts and large-scale commercial properties. No matter the particular project parameters, each design solution considers material richness, attention to detail and respect for both budgetary concerns and site constraints.

Ken and Alec's unwavering dedication to exceeding client expectations and their commitment to facilitating a consistently successful construction and development process have resulted in timeless landscape designs that are beautiful and increase property value. The firm's client commitment is resolute, and the principals maintain that clients should never compromise on their desires because a talented landscape architect can figure out how to meet those wishes without the design feeling forced or contrived.

LAND PLUS ASSOCIATES, LTD.

"Successful land plans are perfected by the creative resolution of broad planning concepts with the design of individual components."

—Alec Michaelides

RIGHT: For a client seeking a casual backyard oasis, we were tasked with designing around 100-year-old oak trees. We used Pennsylvania bluestone for the pool coping and paving along with Tennessee fieldstone for the walls, which harmonize with the buff stucco tone of the home.
Photograph © Jean A. Carnet, Carnet Communications

PREVIOUS PAGES: The pool and pavilion's design synthesizes with the Georgian architectural style of the home, particularly the continuation of brick and use of boxwood hedges; perennial plantings to the rear soften the rigid structure of the hardscape. When working with a classic landscape design, we tend to minimize the amount of flashy plant materials and instead use varying leaf textures and shades of green.
Photograph © Robert Thien, Inc.

ABOVE: Providing the primary backyard access from the front yard, the side yard area represents an opportunity to turn a leftover space into one of delight and interest. The combination of stepping stones and richness of plant materials and textures make it the perfect shade garden.

FACING PAGE TOP: We designed the koi pond, an increasingly popular feature among homeowners, to serve as a focal point from the screened porch and a transition element to the guesthouse. Native Tennessee fieldstone boulders afford the ideal ambience while the greenery above the large rock is actually a biofilter that helps clean the water for the fish.

FACING PAGE BOTTOM: Just left of the koi pond sit the guesthouse and cabana, which exemplifies how the thoughtful design and layout of functional yet engaging outdoor furnishings can create a charming setting.
Photographs © Jean A. Carnet, Carnet Communications

ABOVE: We used a palette of brick and Tennessee fieldstone to complement the English manor-style home, which dictated that the exterior elements, although newly built, have an established feeling to them. The retaining wall separating the pool and the formal area above features a fountain element that pours into a fish pond.

FACING PAGE TOP: We designed the ironwork and gates to play off the home's English manor architecture while providing a gateway to the backyard from the front of the house. The motor court beyond is screened by six-foot-tall courtyard walls.

FACING PAGE BOTTOM LEFT: The entryway from the motor court to the vehicular garden includes ironwork designed to support cherry laurel hedges on either side; the hedges are effectively being trained to grow over the gate.

FACING PAGE BOTTOM RIGHT: Iron fretwork is inset into a charming wooden door that serves as an exterior gate to the motor court from the front yard.
Photographs © Robert Thien, Inc.

"Careful consideration of scale and proportion allows architectural and site opportunities to be seamlessly woven."

—Alec Michaelides

ABOVE: An ethereal outdoor setting features a pair of benches flanked by an enchanting perennial garden, a large mass of tardiva hydrangeas, pink-flowering crape myrtles and a compelling fountain made entirely from lead.

FACING PAGE TOP: A reflecting pond is the focal point from the main center of the 200-acre north Georgia estate property; the pond terminates at a pair of decorative wooden gates, which unfold to the rest of the property.

FACING PAGE BOTTOM LEFT: We designed the garden pavilion to take advantage of the property's topography; because the pavilion is elevated above the rear yard, views from within extend out over the property and beyond the walls.

FACING PAGE BOTTOM RIGHT: The 100-foot-long rose arbor, fashioned from Tennessee fieldstone and western red cedar, concludes at a remarkable fountain that is part of a winsome outdoor setting.
Photographs © Jean A. Carnet, Carnet Communications

"Regardless of a property's size, there must be a comprehensive master plan that links the house to the landscape."

—Alec Michaelides

ABOVE: For the secondary entrance used by the owners' friends, we chose two large stone planters to create a more distinguished appearance.

FACING PAGE TOP: The limestone urn is the focal point of the kitchen garden, which includes a grill, table and chairs and connects directly to the kitchen. An English bench backs up against the bay window while clipped hedges add structure and year-round interest to the herb garden.

FACING PAGE BOTTOM: A teak bench provides a place to enjoy the large perennial garden that functions as the backdrop to the motor court.
Photographs © Jean A. Carnet, Carnet Communications

MICHAEL JACKSON LANDSCAPE

Norcross, Georgia

"The most important element of a successful landscape is the proper installation of drainage, soils and watering systems. If those aren't in place and working together, you're planting a short-term garden."

—Michael Jackson

ABOVE & FACING PAGE: Even if they're not necessarily into gardening, people always seem to get really excited when it's time to design the landscape and select trees, plants and flowers. I understand how they feel because my favorite part of the profession is seeking out and acquiring special plant material—35-foot-tall oaks, mature Japanese maples, interestingly shaped trees—that simply aren't available at nurseries. But there is so much more to a successful landscape than plant selection; you have to create the perfect environment underground.
Above photograph by Michael Jackson
Facing page photograph by Robert Thien

"There's an art and a science in knowing what it takes to create an environment where plant life will thrive."

—Michael Jackson

ABOVE & FACING PAGE: Our first step on any project is preparing the ground: excavating clay, incorporating a special blend of soil—we like to use humus, granite sand, lime and manure—and of course getting the irrigation and drainage systems designed and in place. Although people don't usually think about the sub-grade work, it's critical to a garden's success. For the English Country-style home, we brought in about 300 cubic yards of blended soil mix. The soil mix blended with the native soil provides good drainage and nutrients that enhance the plants' root systems, prevent root rot and allow gardens and lawns to drain as efficiently as putting greens so that they can be enjoyed right after rainfall. Our expertise in this area carries from rooftop gardens to clay tennis courts and beyond; we like to make everything as interconnected and efficient as possible.

Above & facing page bottom photographs by John Umberger
Facing page top photograph by Michael Jackson

"If you want a truly healthy garden, you have to be willing to do whatever it takes to set up an environment of luxury living—from replacing several tons of dirt to drilling wells."

—Michael Jackson

LEFT: There's a really nice transition from the formal garden to the freeform pool to the wooded area beyond, and the landscaping is what ties the whole living space together. The area by the house has almost full sun, but further out the yard is heavily shaded—a custom irrigation system with nearly 40 carefully planned zones sets the scene for plants to flourish. With dogwood, azaleas, rhododendron, hydrangeas and mountain laurel, the backyard feels like a park. I've spent the last two decades developing strong relationships with the area's best landscape architects, designers, lighting specialists and other industry professionals; it's really a pleasure to collaborate with these creative minds to plan out such special projects and bring them to life.

Photograph by Michael Jackson

"If it's done right, a home's landscaping can look completely mature, as if it's always been there, within a year or two of the initial planting."

—Michael Jackson

TOP: No garden is complete without a boxwood element; even whimsical settings need an anchoring element of formality. Boxwoods are like extensions of the architecture, living walls that provide a beautiful frame for free-flowing perennials.
Photograph by Robert Thien

BOTTOM: The most effective way to make a new home feel established in the neighborhood and integrated with its site is through mature trees; if the site doesn't offer those natural amenities, we bring them in. We like to source trees fairly close to home for climate compatibility and recommend oaks and other slow-growing, hearty species. It's best to transplant in dormant months, but we've developed systems that are successful year-round. About eight weeks before the big move, we begin root pruning the tree and feeding it organic stimulants; while that's going on, we're preparing the new site with a sophisticated drainage and irrigation system. When we're ready to uproot the tree and replant it, we bring in a 90-ton crane and a skilled rigging crew. It takes at least half a day to get a 20,000-pound tree into its new location.
Photograph by Michael Jackson

FACING PAGE: The landscape architect was looking for small, formal, pleached trees for the courtyard garden. After some searching, we sourced some single-trunked crape myrtles with rounded heads that fit the description. These were planted in a pea gravel bed, which allowed the area around the trees to be used for garden entertaining. The Italian villa style really drove the look and feel of the landscape design.
Top photograph by Michael Jackson
Bottom photograph © Jean A. Carnet, Carnet Communications

INDIGO POOL & SPA

Lake Oconee, Georgia

"It's important to ask the right questions and really get to know the homeowners so that the design not only meets their specific needs but is a reflection of their distinct personality."

—Jimbo Brown

ABOVE & FACING PAGE: Magnificent waterfalls, lush landscaping, elegant lighting and mesmerizing fountains; many people envision these elements when they dream of a vacation at a posh resort. With a mission to transform backyards into a private oasis, we brought these luxury amenities to life through artistic and personalized aquatic escapes.
Photographs by Blair Brown

"By creating an ambience of gentle water sounds, we are creating total aquatic experiences of relaxation. The audibility of the design is just as important as the way the pool appears."

—Jimbo Brown

RIGHT & FACING PAGE: My world-traveled homeowners have been exposed to the best and will only accept the highest quality in design and materials. Many have such original requests for us and while we always take into consideration the architecture of their home, our goal is to create a unique captivating design. Whether crafting or rehabilitating spaces for entertaining or relaxing, we provide endless options and structural designs. From intimate and classic pools to large-scale projects that include grand amenities such as swim-up bars with underwater granite bar stools, infinity edges, fountains and custom-designed glass tile—attention to detail is our priority.

Photographs by Blair Brown

"A masterful, innovative custom swimming pool creates an extended living space into the backyard, an area to enjoy year-round that—if too cold to swim in—is nevertheless absolutely beautiful to look at."

—Jimbo Brown

ABOVE: Built specifically for a family with two children, the recreational pool has a diving rock and a 10-inch-deep shallow area for the kids to play in or for adults to set up loungechairs and relax. The entire family can fit in the full-size circular spa with massaging jets and watch a flat screen television installed in the patio wall.
Photograph by Bryan Redding

FACING PAGE: Because all of our pools are behind custom-designed homes with amazing architecture, we often collaborate closely with house and landscape architects. For example, an infinity-edge swimming pool—used on lots with good inclines—creates a large waterfall on the backside while maximizing the view. For a house built with entertainment in mind, the actual pillars rise out of the pool, dissolving the veil between indoor and outdoor spaces, and a black granite bar with matching black granite underwater barstools invites the party outside. Or to complement a lake on the opposite side of a house, the pool extends the lake's essence through an oversized tanning ledge with umbrella insert and interior of cobalt blue glass beads to match Italian travertine coping. So many parameters must be taken into consideration.
Photographs by Blair Brown

DOUGLAS OLIVER LANDSCAPE LIGHTING

Marietta, Georgia

"The evening hours are when most people are home with friends and family. It is essential that the lighting is designed to allow them to experience the beauty and charm of their property at that important time."

—Douglas Oliver

ABOVE & FACING PAGE: A well-conceived and professionally executed lighting plan creates warmth and intimacy. Highlighting of unique architectural elements, together with the warm illumination of this reflecting pool, balances nicely with the subtle lighting of the arrival court and surrounding landscape environment.
Photographs © Jean A. Carnet, Carnet Communications

"Interesting people, exciting places and fascinating projects provide a broad spectrum of creative experiences and design inspirations."

—Douglas Oliver

ABOVE: Illumination of the trees, landscape and fountain creates dramatic and interesting reflections in the water. With sensitive, creative lighting, the city garden is transformed into a magical nighttime environment, an atmosphere of tranquility and beauty.

FACING PAGE: Thoughtfully designed lighting transforms environments from daytime activity into areas for evening enjoyment. Subtle illumination of the trees and landscape can have an amazing effect, enhancing the homeowners' appreciation of the function and beauty of their property after dark.

Photographs by Jamey Guy

"It is very important to mix the old in with the new in order to create a garden that is lived in and loved in."

—Kelly Revels

ABOVE: We feel containers should be looked at as artistic expressions of their environment. An antique olive oil jar amidst a loose entry courtyard acts as a focal point to direct guests and friends to the main entrance. Using antique containers in the garden is one of our signature looks. In the marsh garden, we tucked moss-covered creatures and filled them with a variety of succulents to add personality to the outdoor dining area.

FACING PAGE: At the entrance to an oceanfront home, we created a foyer of flora by containing it with hedges and borders. Using a mixture of annuals and perennials in a vibrant color palette, we have designed a whimsical outdoor room instead of a traditional courtyard.
Photographs by Benjamin Galland, H20 Creative Group

"Adding containers in the landscape with height and color adds depth and interest to any garden— a nice contrast to the formal architecture."

—Bryce Vann Frazier

TOP: A mixture of antique Hungarian olive jars and Italian terracotta containers filled with a rustic mix of plant material gives the new home an instant historic feel and serves as the perfect opportunity to showcase true container gardening.

BOTTOM: We have taken a traditional archway entrance off of a tropical pool courtyard and offset it with a mix of formality and texture. The broad leaf of the bird of paradise softens the entryway while an architectural topiary and a loose fern pull the eye toward the door.

FACING PAGE: In order to tie the formality of riverfront landscape back to its natural environment, we planted a trio of containers in nature's color palette with varying heights of topiaries.
Photographs by Benjamin Galland, H20 Creative Group

WORTHY POOLS AND SPAS

St. Simons, Georgia

"The perfect swimming pool brings two things to a home: beauty and fun."

—Betsy Worthy

ABOVE & FACING PAGE: Because we live and work in such a beautiful part of coastal Georgia, the pools that we design and build are meant to incorporate the natural surroundings. Whether the project is on the beach or set against giant live oaks on the marsh, we can achieve the most naturally integrated settings.

Photographs courtesy of Worthy Pools and Spas

"Water features can turn a simple backyard into something amazing."

—Henry Worthy

ABOVE: Our clients want their pools and spas to be an oasis of relaxation. Whether they are entertaining friends poolside or splashing around with the children, we take the anxiety out of the equation.

FACING PAGE: Twenty years in the business and 1,000 pools later, we can look at an empty lot and envision the layout possibilities. We know that this is the most critical time to listen to the client's visions and tie them in with all the aspects of the project. The results? Seamless and amazing.
Photographs courtesy of Worthy Pools and Spas

perspectives
ON DESIGN

GEORGIA TEAM

ASSOCIATE PUBLISHER: Emily Ratchford

GRAPHIC DESIGNER: Kendall Muellner

EDITOR: Michael C. McConnell

MANAGING PRODUCTION COORDINATOR: Kristy Randall

HEADQUARTERS TEAM

PUBLISHER: Brian G. Carabet

PUBLISHER: John A. Shand

EXECUTIVE PUBLISHER: Phil Reavis

DIRECTOR OF DEVELOPMENT & DESIGN: Beth Benton Buckley

PUBLICATION & CIRCULATION MANAGER: Lauren B. Castelli

SENIOR GRAPHIC DESIGNER: Emily A. Kattan

GRAPHIC DESIGNER: Ashley Rodges

MANAGING EDITOR: Rosalie Z. Wilson

EDITOR: Anita M. Kasmar

EDITOR: Jennifer Nelson

EDITOR: Sarah Tangney

PRODUCTION COORDINATOR: Maylin Medina

PRODUCTION COORDINATOR: Drea Williams

ADMINISTRATIVE MANAGER: Carol Kendall

ADMINISTRATIVE ASSISTANT: Beverly Smith

CLIENT SUPPORT COORDINATOR: Amanda Mathers

PANACHE PARTNERS, LLC
CORPORATE HEADQUARTERS
1424 Gables Court
Plano, TX 75075
469.246.6060
www.panache.com
www.panachedesign.com

index

Land Plus Associates, Ltd., page 246

Indigo Pool & Spa, page 266

Douglas Oliver Landscape Lighting, page 272

THE PANACHE COLLECTION

CREATING SPECTACULAR PUBLICATIONS FOR DISCERNING READERS

Dream Homes Series
An Exclusive Showcase of the Finest Architects, Designers and Builders

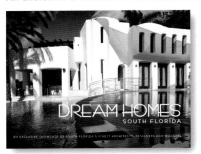

Carolinas
Chicago
Coastal California
Colorado
Deserts
Florida
Georgia
Los Angeles
Metro New York
Michigan
Minnesota
New England
New Jersey

Northern California
Ohio & Pennsylvania
Pacific Northwest
Philadelphia
South Florida
Southwest
Tennessee
Texas
Washington, D.C.

Spectacular Homes Series
An Exclusive Showcase of the Finest Interior Designers

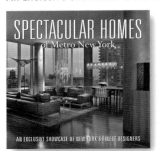

California
Carolinas
Chicago
Colorado
Florida
Georgia
Heartlands
London
Michigan
Minnesota
New England

New York
Ohio & Pennsylvania
Pacific Northwest
Philadelphia
South Florida
Southwest
Tennessee
Texas
Toronto
Washington, D.C.
Western Canada

Perspectives on Design Series
Design Philosophies Expressed by Leading Professionals

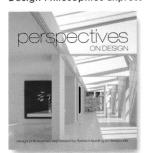

California
Carolinas
Chicago
Colorado
Florida
Georgia

Great Lakes
Minnesota
New England
Pacific Northwest
Southwest

Art of Celebration Series
The Making of a Gala

Chicago
Georgia
Midwest
New York
Philadelphia
South Florida
Southern California
Southwest
Texas
Wine Country

Spectacular Wineries Series
A Captivating Tour of Established, Estate and Boutique Wineries

California's Central Coast
Napa Valley
New York
Sonoma County

Specialty Titles
The Finest in Unique Luxury Lifestyle Publications

Cloth and Culture: Ruth E. Funk
Distinguished Inns of North America
Extraordinary Homes California
Geoffrey Bradfield Ex Arte
Into the Earth: A Wine Cave Renaissance
Spectacular Golf of Colorado
Spectacular Golf of Texas
Spectacular Hotels
Spectacular Restaurants of Texas
Visions of Design

City by Design Series
An Architectural Perspective

Atlanta
Charlotte
Chicago
Dallas
Denver
Orlando
Phoenix
San Francisco
Texas

PanacheDesign.com
Where the Design Industry's Finest Professionals Gather, Share and Inspire

PANACHEdesign

PanacheDesign.com overflows with innovative ideas from leading architects, builders, interior designers and other specialists. A gallery of design photographs and library of advice-oriented articles are among the comprehensive site's offerings.

PANACHE PARTNERS, LLC ▪ 1424 GABLES COURT ▪ PLANO, TEXAS 75075 ▪ 469.246.6060 ▪ WWW.PANACHE.COM